DISAPPOINTMENT WITH GOD

Philip Yancey is one of the most significant Christian writers of our day. His books, which explore the meaning of suffering, have won numerous awards and have sold millions of copies worldwide.

He is editor-at-large of *Christianity Today*, and a frequent speaker at major Christian conferences and events in the United States and in the United Kingdom.

Philip Yancey is married to Janet, and they live in Colorado.

For my brother,
who is still disappointed

Also available from Marshall Pickering
by the same author

Where Is God When It Hurts?

and with Paul Brand

Fearfully and wonderfully made
Pain: The Gift Nobody Wants

Forthcoming in 1995

The Jesus I Never Knew

Disappointment With God

Three Questions No One Asks Aloud

Philip Yancey

Marshall Pickering
An Imprint of HarperCollinsPublishers

Marshall Pickering is an imprint of
HarperCollins*Religious*
Part of HarperCollins*Publishers*
77–85 Fulham Palace Road, London W6 8JB

First published in the USA in 1988 by Zondervan Publishing House
Published in Great Britain in 1989 under the title
Seeing in the Dark by Marshall Morgan & Scott,
a forerunner of Marshall Pickering
This edition published in 1995 by Marshall Pickering

3 5 7 9 10 8 6 4

A catalogue record for this book
is available from the British Library

ISBN 0 551 02972 2

Printed and bound in Great Britain

Contents

Foreword

AFTER I HAD BEGUN WORK on this project, I received phone calls from a few people in my church who had heard about it. "Is it true you're writing a book about disappointment with God?" the callers would ask. "If so, I'd like to talk. I haven't told anyone before, but my life as a Christian has included times of great disappointment." I did interview some of those callers, and their stories helped set the direction of this book.

I found that for many people there is a large gap between what they *expect* from their Christian faith and what they actually experience. From a steady diet of books, sermons, and personal testimonies, all promising triumph and success, they learn to expect dramatic evidence of God working in their lives. If they do not see such evidence, they feel disappointment, betrayal, and often guilt. As one woman said, "I kept hearing the phrase, 'personal relationship with Jesus Christ.' But I found to my dismay that it is unlike any other personal relationship. I never saw God, or heard him, or felt him, or experienced the most basic ingredients of a relationship. Either there's something wrong with what I was told, or there's something wrong with me."

Disappointment occurs when the actual experience of something falls far short of what we anticipate. For that reason, the first half of this book explores the Bible to see what we can rightfully expect from God. I hesitated to start there since I know that some people, especially disappointed people, have little tolerance for the Bible. But what better place to begin than by letting God speak for himself? I tried to rid myself of preconceptions and read the Bible like a story, with a "plot." What I found there astonished me. It was very different from the story I had been told most of my life.

Actually, I set out to write two different books, and did so; but I ended up putting them both between the same covers. Book II moves to more practical, existential issues and applies the ideas I have developed to actual situations—the kinds of situations that foster disappointment with God. Ultimately, I concluded that the two approaches belonged in the same book; either would be incomplete on its own.

Once as I explained this project to a friend, he frowned and shook his head. "I guess I've never tried to psychoanalyze God before," he said. I hope that's not what I'm attempting! But I do wish to understand God better, to learn why he sometimes acts in such mysterious ways—or does not seem to act at all.

A few words of caution, however. This is not a book of apologetics, so I will not travel the path of pointing out evidences for God. Others have done that effectively, and, besides, I am dealing with doubts that are more emotional than intellectual. Disappointment implies a hoped-for relationship that somehow has not worked out.

Nor will I debate the question, "Does God ever perform miracles?" I take for granted that he has supernatural power and has used it. Yes, God can intervene; so why doesn't he do so more often? Why handicap himself among sincere skeptics who would like to believe, if only they had a sign? Why permit injustice and suffering to thrive on earth? Why aren't God's interventions "ordinaries" rather than "miracles"?

One last caution: by no means am I presenting a balanced view of the Christian faith. I am, after all, writing for people who have, at one time or another, heard the silence of God. Studying someone like Job as an example of faith is a little like studying the history of civilization by examining only the wars. On the other hand, there are many Christian books that leave out any mention of the wars and promise nothing but victory. This is a book about faith, but it looks at faith through the eyes of those who doubt.

And finally, I should explain the way I have chosen to handle

Bible references. I resisted putting them in footnotes or parentheses within the text: that creates an awkwardness in reading not unlike listening to someone with a stutter. Instead, I have indicated the sources of direct citations at the end of each chapter. True sleuths should be able to track down the correct passage.

Awake, O Lord! Why do you sleep?
Rouse yourself! Do not reject us forever.
Why do you hide your face?

—Psalm 44:23–24

BOOK I

GOD WITHIN
THE SHADOWS

*You do not have to sit outside in the dark.
If, however, you want to look at the stars,
you will find that darkness is required.
The stars neither require it nor demand it.*
                                    —Annie Dillard

Part One

Hearing the Silence

Chapter 1

A Fatal Error

E VER SINCE my book *Where Is God When It Hurts?* was published, I have received letters from people disappointed with God.

A young mother wrote that her joy had turned to bitterness and grief when she delivered a daughter with *spina bifida,* a birth defect that leaves the spinal cord exposed. In page after page of tiny, spidery script she recounted how medical bills had soaked up the family savings and how her marriage had cracked apart as her husband came to resent all the time she devoted to their sick child. As her life crumbled around her, she was beginning to doubt what she had once believed about a loving God. Did I have any advice?

A homosexual spilled out his story gradually, in a succession of letters. For more than a decade he had sought a "cure" for his sexual orientation, trying charismatic healing services, Christian support groups, and chemical treatment. He even underwent a form of aversion therapy in which psychologists applied electrical shocks to his genitals when he responded to erotic photos of men. Nothing worked. Finally he surrendered to a life of gay promiscuity. He still writes me occasionally. He insists that he wants to follow God but feels disqualified because of his peculiar curse.

A young woman wrote, with some embarrassment, about her ongoing depression. She has no reason to be depressed, she said. She is healthy, earns a good salary, and has a stable family background. Yet most days when she wakes up she cannot think of a single reason to go on living. She no longer cares about life or God, and when she prays, she wonders if anyone is really listening.

These and other letters I have received over the years all lead up to the same basic question, phrased in different ways. It goes something like this: "Your book is about physical pain. But what about pain like mine? Where is God when I hurt emotionally? What does the Bible say about that?" I answer the letters as best I can, sadly conscious of the inadequacy of words on paper. Can a word, any word, ever heal a wound? And I must confess that after reading these anguished accounts I ask the very same questions. Where is God in our emotional pain? Why does he so often disappoint us?

Disappointment with God does not come only in dramatic circumstances. For me, it also edges unexpectedly into the mundaneness of everyday life. I remember one night last winter, a cold, raw Chicago night. The wind was howling, and sleet slanted out of the skies, coating the streets with darkly shining ice. That night my car stalled in a rather ominous neighborhood. As I raised the hood and hunched over the engine, the sleet stinging my back like tiny pebbles, I prayed over and over, *Please help me get this car started.*

No amount of fiddling with wires and tubes and cables would start the car, and so I spent the next hour in a dilapidated diner waiting for a tow truck. Sitting on a plastic chair, my drenched clothes forming a widening pool of water around me, I wondered what God thought about my plight. I would miss a scheduled meeting that night and would probably waste many hours over the next few days trying to wring fair, honest work out of a service station set up to prey upon stranded motorists. Did God even care about my frustration or the waste of energy and money?

Like the woman embarrassed over her depression, I feel ashamed even to mention such an unanswered prayer. It seems petty and selfish, maybe even stupid, to pray for a car to start. But I have found that petty disappointments tend to accumulate over time, undermining my faith with a lava flow of doubt. I start to wonder whether God cares about everyday details—about me. I am tempted to pray less often, having concluded in advance that it won't matter. Or will it? My emotions and my faith waver. Once those doubts seep in, I am even less prepared for times of major crisis. A neighbor is dying of cancer; I pray diligently for her. But even as I pray, I wonder. Can God be trusted? If so many small prayers go unanswered, what about the big ones?

One morning in a motel room I switched on the television and the square, jowly face of a well-known evangelist filled the screen. "I'm mad at God!" he said, glowering. It was a remarkable confession from a man who had built his career around the notion of "seed faith" and absolute confidence in God's personal concern. But God had let him down, he said, and went on to explain. God had commanded him to build a large ministry complex; and yet the project proved to be a financial disaster, forcing him to sell off properties and cut back programs. He had kept his part of the bargain, but God had not.

A few weeks later I again saw the evangelist on television, this time exuding faith and optimism. He leaned toward the camera, his craggy face splitting into a big grin, and jabbed his finger toward a million viewers. "Something *good* is going to happen to you this week!" he said, coaxing three syllables out of the word "good." He was at his salesman best, utterly convincing. A few days later, however, I heard on the news that his son had committed suicide. I could not help wondering what the evangelist said to God in his prayers that fateful week.

Such struggles seem almost to mock the triumphant slogans

about God's love and personal concern that I often hear in Christian churches. Yet no one is immune to the downward spiral of disappointment. It happens to people like the televangelist and to people like the letter writers, and it happens to ordinary Christians: first comes disappointment, then a seed of doubt, then a response of anger or betrayal. We begin to question whether God is trustworthy, whether we can really stake our lives on him.

3

I have been thinking about this topic of disappointment with God for a long time, but I hesitated to write about it for two reasons. First, I knew I would have to confront questions that have no easy answers—that may, in fact, have no answers. And second, I did not want to write a book that would, by focusing on failure, dampen anyone's faith.

Some Christians, I know, would reject the phrase "disappointment with God" out of hand. Such a notion is all wrong, they say. Jesus promised that faith the size of a grain of mustard seed can move mountains; that anything can happen if two or three gather together in prayer. The Christian life is a life of victory and triumph. God wants us happy, healthy, and prosperous, and any other state simply indicates a lack of faith.

During a visit among people who believe exactly this, I finally reached the decision to write this book. I was investigating the topic of physical healing for a magazine assignment, and the research led me to a rather infamous church headquartered in rural Indiana. I had learned of the church from a *Chicago Tribune* series and from a special report on ABC's "Nightline" program.

Members of this church believed that simple faith could heal any disease and that to look elsewhere for help—for example, to medical doctors—demonstrated a lack of faith in God. The *Tribune* articles told of parents who had looked on helplessly as their children fought losing battles with meningitis or pneumonia or a common flu virus—diseases that easily could have been treated. On a map of the United States, a *Tribune* artist had drawn tiny tombstone symbols to mark where people had died after refusing medical treatment in accordance with church teaching. There were fifty-two tombstones in all.

According to the reports, pregnant women in that church died in childbirth at a rate eight times the national average, and young children were three times more likely to die. Yet the church was growing and had established branches in nineteen states and five foreign countries.

I visited the mother church in Indiana on a sweltering August day. Heat waves shimmied off the asphalt roads, and parched brown cornstalks drooped in the fields. The building sat unmarked in the midst of one of those cornfields—huge, isolated, like a misplaced barn. In the parking lot I had to talk my way past two ushers with walkie-talkies; the church was nervous about publicity, especially since former members had recently filed lawsuits.

I suppose I expected a sign of fanaticism during the service: a swooning, hypnotic sermon delivered by a Jim Jones–type preacher. I saw nothing like that. For ninety minutes, seven hundred of us sitting in a large semicircle sang hymns and studied the Bible.

I was among simple people. The women wore dresses or skirts, no slacks, and used little makeup. The men, dressed in shirts and ties, sat with their families and helped keep the children in line.

Children were far more conspicuous here than in most churches; they were everywhere. Keeping quiet for ninety minutes stretches the limits of a small child's endurance, and I watched the parents try to cope. Coloring books abounded. Mothers played games with their children's fingers. Some had brought along a treasure trove of toys in oversized pocketbooks.

If I had come looking for sensationalism, I went away disappointed. I had seen a slice of old-fashioned Americana where the traditional family was still alive and well. Parents there loved their children as much as any parents on earth.

And yet—the map with the tiny tombstones leaped to mind—some of those same parents had sat by the bedsides of their dying youngsters and done nothing. One father told the *Tribune* of his prayer vigil as he watched his fifteen-month-old son battle a fever for two weeks. The illness first caused deafness, then blindness. The pastor of the church urged even more faith and persuaded the father not to call a doctor. The next day the boy was dead. An autopsy revealed that he had died from an easily treatable form of meningitis.

By and large, the members of the Indiana church do not blame God for their miseries, or at least they do not admit to doing so. Instead, they blame themselves for weak faith. Meanwhile, the tombstones multiply.

I went away from that Sunday service with a profound conviction that what we think about God and believe about God matters—*really* matters—as much as anything in life matters. Those people were not ogres or child-murderers, and yet several dozen of their children had died because of an error (I believe) in theology. (Actually, the teaching of the Indiana church is not so different from what I hear in many evangelical churches and on religious television and radio; they simply apply the extravagant promises of faith more consistently.)

Because of those sincere people in Indiana, along with the questioning people who had written to me, I decided to confront issues I am sorely tempted to avoid. Thus, this book of theology. Not a technical book by any means, but a book about the nature of God and why he sometimes acts in puzzling ways and sometimes does not act.

We dare not confine theology to seminary coffee shops where professors and students play mental badminton. It affects all of us. Some people lose their faith because of a sharp sense of disappointment with God. They expect God to act a certain way, and God "lets them down." Others may not lose their faith, but they too experience a form of disappointment. They believe God will intervene, they pray for a miracle, and their prayers come back unanswered. Fifty-two times, at least, it happened that way in the Indiana church.

Chapter 2

Up in Smoke

ONE AFTERNOON my phone rang and the caller identified himself as a theology student at Wheaton College Graduate School. "My name is Richard," he said. "We haven't met, but I feel a kinship with you because of some of your writings. Do you have a minute?"

Richard proceeded to tell me about his life. He had become a Christian as a university student when an InterVarsity worker befriended him and introduced him to the faith. Yet Richard hardly talked like a new Christian. Although he asked for my recommendations of Christian books, I found that he had already read each one I mentioned. We had a pleasant, wandering conversation, and not until the end of the call did I learn his real purpose in contacting me.

"I hate to bother you with this," he said nervously. "I know you're probably busy, but there is one favor I'd like to ask. You see, I wrote this paper on the Book of Job, and my professor told me I should make a book out of it. Is there a chance you could take a look and see what you think?"

I said yes, and the manuscript arrived within a few days. In truth, I did not expect much. Graduate school papers do not normally make compelling reading, and I doubted whether a relatively recent convert could come up with fresh insights on the daunting Book of Job. But I was wrong. The manuscript showed real promise, and over the next few months Richard and I discussed by phone and mail how the paper could be reshaped into book form.

A year later, with a finished manuscript and a signed contract in hand, Richard called to ask if I would write a foreword. I had still never met Richard, but I liked his enthusiasm, and he had written a book I could easily endorse.

Six months passed, during which the book went through final editing and revision. Then, shortly before its publication date, Richard called yet again. His voice sounded different: tense, edgy. To my surprise he fended off questions about his forthcoming book. "I need to see you, Philip," he said. "There's something I feel obligated to tell you, and it should be in person. Could I come over some afternoon this week?"

Hot, hazy rays of sunlight streamed into my third-floor apartment. The open French doors had no screens, and flies buzzed in and out of the room. Richard, dressed in white tennis shorts and a T-shirt, sat on a couch across from me. Sweat glistened on his forehead. He had driven for an hour in heavy Chicago traffic for this meeting, and he first gulped down a glass of iced tea, trying to cool off.

Richard was lean and in good physical shape—"pure ectomorph," as an aerobics instructor might say. A bony face and short-cropped hair gave him the severe, intense look of a God-haunted monk. If body language speaks, his was voluble: his fists clenched and unclenched, his tanned legs crossed and uncrossed, and his facial muscles often tightened with tension.

He skipped the small talk. "You've a right to be furious with me," he began. "I don't blame you a bit if you feel snookered."

I had no idea what he meant. "About what?"

"Well, it's like this. The book you helped me with—it's coming out next month, including your foreword. But the truth is, I don't believe what I wrote in that book anymore, and I feel I owe you an explanation."

He paused for a moment, and I watched the lines of tension working in his jaw. "I hate God!" he suddenly blurted out. "No, I don't mean that. I don't even believe in God."

I said nothing. In fact, I said very little for the next three hours as Richard told me his story, beginning with his parents' breakup. "I did everything I could to prevent the divorce," he said. "I'd just become a Christian at the university, and I was naive enough to believe that God cared. I prayed nonstop day and night that they'd get back together. I even dropped out of school for a while and went home to try to salvage my family. I thought I was doing God's will, but I think I made everything worse. It was my first bitter experience with unanswered prayer.

"I transferred to Wheaton College to learn more about the faith. I figured I must be doing something wrong. At Wheaton I met people who used phrases like 'I spoke with God,' and 'the Lord told me.' I sometimes talked like that too, but never without a twitch of guilt. Did the Lord really tell me anything? I never heard a voice or had any proof of God I could see or touch. Yet I longed for that kind of closeness.

"Each time I faced a crucial decision I would read the Bible and pray for guidance, like you're supposed to. Whenever I felt right about the decision, I would act on it. But, I swear, I ended up making the wrong choice every time. Just when I really thought I understood God's will, then it would backfire on me."

Street noises drifted in, and I could hear neighbors going up and down the stairs, but these sounds did not distract Richard. He kept talking, and I nodded occasionally, though I still did not understand the reason for his almost violent outburst against God. Lots of families break up; lots of prayers go unanswered. What was the true source of his molten rage?

He next told me about a job opportunity that had fallen through. The employer reneged on a promise to him and hired someone less deserving, leaving Richard with school debts and no source of income. About the same time, Richard's fiancee jilted him. With no warning she broke off contact, refusing to give any explanation for her abrupt change of heart. Sharon, the fiancee, had played a key role in Richard's spiritual growth, and as she left him, he felt some of his faith leach away as well. They had often prayed together about their future; now those prayers seemed like cruel jokes.

Richard also had a series of physical problems, which only added to his sense of helplessness and depression. Wounds of rejection, suffered when his parents had separated, seemed to reopen. Had God merely been stringing him along—like Sharon? He visited a pastor for advice. He felt like a drowning man, he said. He wanted to trust God, but whenever he reached out he grasped a fistful of air. Why should he keep believing in a God so apparently unconcerned about his well-being?

The pastor was barely sympathetic, and Richard got the clear impression that his own complaints did not measure up to the man's normal fare of broken marriages, cancer patients, alcoholics, and parents of wayward children. "When something straightens out with your girlfriend, you'll straighten out with God, too," the pastor said with a condescending smile.

To Richard, the problems were anything but minor. He could not understand why a loving heavenly Father would let him suffer such disappointment. No earthly father would treat his child like that. He continued going to church, but inside him a hard lump of cynicism began forming, a tumor of doubt. The theology he had learned in school and had written about in his book no longer worked for him.

"It was odd," Richard told me, "but the more anger I directed at God, the more energy I seemed to gain. I realized that for the last several years I had shrunken inside myself. Now, as I started doubting, and even hating the school and other Christians around me, I felt myself coming back to life."

One night something snapped. Richard attended a Sunday evening church service where he heard the usual testimonies and praise, but one report in particular rankled him. Earlier that week a plane carrying nine missionaries had crashed in the Alaskan outback, killing all aboard. The pastor solemnly related the details and then introduced a member of the church who had survived an unrelated plane crash that same week. When the church member finished describing his narrow escape, the congregation responded, "Praise the Lord!"

"Lord, we thank you for bringing our brother to safety and for having your guardian angels watch over him," the pastor prayed. "And please be with the families of those who died in Alaska." That prayer triggered revulsion, something like nausea, in Richard. You can't have it both ways, he thought. If God gets credit for the survivor, he should also get blamed for the casualties. Yet churches never hear testimonies from the grievers. What would the spouses of the dead missionaries say? Would they talk about a "loving Father"?

Richard returned to his apartment greatly agitated. Everything was coming to a head around one question: "Is God even there?" He had not seen convincing evidence.

3

Richard interrupted his story at this point. The sun had strayed behind a large building to the west, gauzily softening the room's shadows and streaks of light. Richard closed his eyes and chewed on his lower lip. He pressed on his eyes with his thumbs, hard. He seemed to be setting a mental picture, as if to get it just right.

"What happened next?" I asked, after a few minutes of silence. "Was that the night you lost your faith?"

He nodded and resumed speaking, but in a subdued tone. "I stayed up late that night, long after my neighbors had gone to bed—I live on a quiet street in the suburbs—and it seemed like I was alone in the world. I sensed something important was about to happen. I was hurt. So many times God had let me down. I hated God, and yet I was afraid too. I was a theology student, right? Maybe God was there and I had it all wrong. How could I know? I went back over my whole Christian experience, from the very beginning.

"I remembered the first flush of faith at the university. I was young then, and vulnerable. Maybe I had just learned a few upbeat phrases and talked myself into believing in 'an abundant life.' Maybe I had been mimicking other people and living off their experiences. Had I deluded myself about God?

"Still, I hesitated to cast aside all that I believed. I felt I had to give God one last chance.

"I prayed that night as earnestly and sincerely as I knew how. I prayed on my knees, and I prayed stretched out flat on the oak floor. 'God! Do you care?' I prayed. 'I don't want to tell you how to run your world, but please give me some sign that you're really there! That's all I ask.'

"For four years I'd been straining for 'a personal relationship with God,' as the phrase goes, and yet God had treated me worse than any of my friends. Now everything narrowed down to one final question: How can you have a personal relationship if you're not sure the other person even exists? With God, I could never be sure.

"I prayed for at least four hours. At times I felt foolish, at times utterly sincere. I had the sensation of stepping off a ledge in the darkness with no idea where I might land. That was up to God.

"Finally, at four o'clock in the morning, I came to my senses. Nothing had happened. God had not responded. Why continue torturing myself? Why not just forget God and get on with life, like most of the rest of the world?

"Instantly I felt a sense of relief and freedom, like I had just passed a final exam or gotten my first driver's license. The struggle was over. My life was my own.

"It seems silly now, but this is what I did next. I picked up my Bible and a couple other Christian books and walked downstairs and out the back door. I shut the door softly behind me, so as not to wake anyone. In the backyard was a brick barbecue grill, and I piled the books on it, sprayed them with lighter fluid, and struck a match. It was a moonless night, and the flames danced high and bright. Bible verses and bits of theology curled, blackened, then broke off in tiny crumbs of ash and floated skyward. My faith was going up with them.

"I made another trip upstairs and brought down another armload of books. I did this maybe eight times over the next hour. Commentaries, seminary textbooks, the rough draft of my book on Job—all of them went up in smoke. I might have burned every book I owned if I hadn't been interrupted by an angry fireman in a yellow rain slicker who ran toward me, shouting, 'What do you think you're doing!' Someone had phoned in an alarm. I fumbled around for an excuse and finally told him I was just burning trash.

"After the fireman had squirted some chemicals on my bonfire and shoveled dirt over it, he let me go. I climbed the stairs and sank into bed, smelling of smoke. It was almost dawn by then, and at last I had peace. A great weight had lifted. I had been honest with myself. Any pretense was gone, and I no longer felt the pressure to believe what I could never be sure of. I felt converted—but converted *from* God."

I'm glad I don't make my living as a professional counselor. When I sit across from someone spilling his guts like Richard did, I never know what to say. I said little that afternoon, and maybe that was best. It would not have helped for me to find fault with the "tests" Richard had devised for God.

He seemed especially concerned about the book on Job due out within the next few weeks. The publisher knew about his change of heart, he said, but the first edition was already on the presses. I assured him my endorsement of the book still held. It was the content of the book I was endorsing, more than his personal attachment. "Besides, I've certainly changed my mind about some things I've written in the last ten years," I told him.

Richard was exhausted after talking so long, but he seemed more relaxed as he stood to leave. "Maybe all my problems started with my study of Job," he said. "I used to love Job—he wasn't afraid to be honest with God. He took God on. I guess the difference between us is what happened at the end. God came through for Job, after all his pain. He didn't come through for me."

Dusk had fallen, and a photocell had already switched on the stairway lights. As Richard shook my hand and disappeared down the steps, I felt very sad. He was young and tanned and healthy. Some would say he had no real reason to despair. But listening to him, watching his hands clenching and the lines of tension in his face, I had recognized at last the source of his rage.

Richard was feeling a pain as great as any that a human being experiences: the pain of betrayal. The pain of a lover who wakes up and suddenly realizes *it's all over*. He had staked his life on God, and God had let him down.

Chapter 3

The Questions No One
Asks Aloud

SOMETIMES the most important questions, those that float in vague suspension for much of our lives, can crystallize in a single moment. Richard's visit provided such a moment for me. In one respect his complaints—broken home, health problems, failed romance, lost job—hardly ranked as world-class disappointments. And yet that night by the barbecue grill he had, with theatrical finality, acted on the doubts that plague almost all of us. Does God really care? If so, why won't he reach down and fix the things that go wrong—at least some of them?

Absorbed in his anger and pain, Richard had not given voice to his doubts in a systematic way; he experienced them more as feelings of betrayal than as matters of faith. As I brooded over our conversation, however, I kept returning to three large questions about God that seemed to lurk just behind the thicket of his feelings. The longer I pondered them, the more I realized that these questions are lodged somewhere inside all of us. Yet few people ask them aloud, for they seem at best impolite, at worst heretical.

Is God unfair? Richard had tried to follow God, but his life fell apart anyway. He could not reconcile his miseries with the biblical promises of rewards and happiness. And what about the people who openly deny God yet prosper anyway? This is an old complaint, as old as Job and the Psalms, but it remains a stumbling block to faith.

Is God silent? Three times, as he faced crucial choices in his education, career, and romance, Richard begged God for clear direction. Each time he thought he had God's will figured out, only to have that choice lead to failure. "What kind of Father is he?" Richard asked. "Does he enjoy watching me fall on my face? I was told that God loves me and has a wonderful plan for my life. Fine. So why doesn't he tell me what that plan is?"

Is God hidden? This question, above all, obsessed Richard. It seemed to him an irreducible minimum, a theological bottom line, that God should somehow prove himself: "How can I have a relationship with a Person I'm not even sure exists?" Yet it seemed that God deliberately hid himself, even from people who sought him out. And when Richard's late-night vigil provoked no response, he simply gave up on God.

I thought about these three questions often on a subsequent writing assignment in South America. In Peru, a missionary pilot flew me to a small Shipibo Indian village. He landed the floatplane, taxied to the riverbank, and guided me along a jungle trail to the main "street" in town: a dirt path surrounded by a dozen huts built on stilts and covered with palm-frond roofs. He had brought me there to show me a thriving, forty-year-old church. But he also showed me a granite marker just off the main path and told me the story of the young missionary who had helped found that church.

When his six-month-old son died from a sudden onset of vomiting and diarrhea, the young missionary seemed to crack. He hewed a marker by hand from local stone—the marker we were looking at—buried the baby's body, and planted a tree beside the grave. At the hottest part of each day, when everyone else sought shade, the missionary walked to the river and hauled back a jug of water for the tree. Then he stood beside the grave, his shadow falling across it, as if to shield it from the blazing equatorial sun. Sometimes he would weep, sometimes pray, and sometimes just stand there with a vacant gaze. His wife, the Indian church members, and other missionaries all tried to comfort him, but to no avail.

Eventually, the missionary himself got sick. His mind wandered; he had constant diarrhea. He was flown to Lima, where doctors probed him for any sign of amoeba or other tropical organisms, but found nothing. None of the drugs they tried were effective. They diagnosed his problem as "hysterical diarrhea" and sent him and his wife back to the United States.

As I stood beside the crumbling granite marker, which the Indian women now used as a place to rest their water pots, I tried to put myself in that young missionary's place. I wondered what he had prayed as he stood there in the noonday sun, and Richard's three questions kept coming to mind. My guide had said the man was tormented by the question of unfairness. His baby had done nothing wrong. The missionary had brought his family to serve God in the jungle—was this their reward? He had also prayed for some sign of God's presence, or at least a word of comfort. But he felt none. As if distrustful of God's own sympathy, the missionary took on a form of sympathetic suffering in his own body.

True atheists do not, I presume, feel disappointed in God. They expect nothing and receive nothing. But those who commit their lives to God, no matter what, instinctively expect something in return. Are those expectations wrong?

I did not see my friend Richard for a long time. I prayed for him regularly, but all my efforts to contact him proved futile. His phone had been disconnected, and I heard he had moved out of the area. His publisher eventually sent me a copy of his book on Job, and it sat on my shelf as a potent warning against writing too hastily on matters of faith.

Then one day, about three years later, I bumped into Richard in downtown Chicago. He looked good: by putting on a little weight and letting his hair grow a few inches longer, he had lost the haunted, severe mien. He seemed glad to see me, and we scheduled a lunch.

"Last time I met with you, I guess I was in the pits," he said with a smile as he joined me in a Mexican restaurant a few days later. "Life is treating me much better now." He had a promising job and had long since put the failed romance behind him.

Soon our conversation turned to God, and it quickly became evident that Richard had not fully recovered. A thick scab of cynicism now covered the wounds, but he was as angry at God as ever.

The waitress poured a fresh cup of coffee, and Richard wrapped both hands around the cup and stared at the dark, steaming liquid. "I've gained some perspective on that crazy period," he said. "I think I've figured out what went wrong. I can tell you the exact hour and minute I began doubting God, and it wasn't at Wheaton or in my room that night I stayed up praying." He then related an incident that had occurred very early in his Christian life.

"One thing bugged me from the very beginning: the notion of faith. It seemed a black hole that could gobble up any honest question. I'd ask the InterVarsity leader about the problem of pain, and he would spout something about faith. 'Believe God whether you feel like it or not,' he'd say. 'The feelings will follow.' I faked it, but I can now see that the feelings never followed. I was just going through the motions.

"Even back then I was searching for hard evidence of God as an alternative to faith. And one day I found it—on television, of all places. While randomly flipping a dial, I came across a mass healing service being conducted by Kathryn Kuhlman. I watched for a few minutes as she brought various people up on the stage and interviewed them. Each one told an amazing story of supernatural healing. Cancer, heart conditions, paralysis—it was like a medical encyclopedia up there.

"As I watched Kuhlman's program, my doubts gradually melted away. At last I had found something real and tangible. Kuhlman asked a musician to sing her favorite song, 'He Touched

Me.' That's what I needed, I thought: a touch, a personal touch from God. She held out that promise, and I lunged for it.

"Three weeks later when Kathryn Kuhlman came to a neighboring state, I skipped classes and traveled half a day to attend one of her meetings. The atmosphere was unbelievably charged—soft organ music in the background; the murmuring sound of people praying aloud, some in strange tongues; and every few minutes a happy interruption when someone would stand and claim, 'I'm healed!'

"One person especially made an impression, a man from Milwaukee who had been carried into the meeting on a stretcher. When he walked—yes, walked—onstage, we all cheered wildly. He told us he was a physician, and I was even more impressed. He had incurable lung cancer, he said, and was told he had six months to live. But now, tonight, he believed God had healed him. He was walking for the first time in months. He felt great. Praise God!

"I wrote down the man's name and practically floated out of that meeting. I had never known such certainty of faith before. My search was over; I had seen proof of a living God in those people on the stage. If he could work tangible miracles in them, then surely he had something wonderful in store for me.

"I wanted contact with the man of faith I had seen at the meeting, so much so that exactly one week later I phoned Directory Assistance in Milwaukee and got the physician's number. When I dialed it, a woman answered the phone. 'May I please speak to Dr. S_____,' I said.

"Long silence. 'Who are you?' she said at last. I figured she was just screening calls from patients or something. I gave my name and told her I admired Dr. S_____ and had wanted to talk to him ever since the Kathryn Kuhlman meeting. I had been very moved by his story, I said.

"Another long silence. Then she spoke in a flat voice, pronouncing each word slowly. 'My . . . husband . . . is . . . dead.' Just that one sentence, nothing more, and she hung up.

"I can't tell you how that devastated me. I was wasted. I half-staggered into the next room, where my sister was sitting. 'Richard, what's wrong?' she asked. 'Are you all right?'

"No, I was not all right. But I couldn't talk about it. I was crying. My mother and sister tried to pry some explanation out of me. But what could I tell them? For me, the certainty I had staked my life on had died with that phone call. A flame had flared bright for one fine, shining week and then gone dark, like a dying star."

Richard stared into his coffee cup. Marimba music playing in the background sounded tinny and jarringly loud. "I don't quite understand," I said. "That happened long before you went to Wheaton and got a theology degree and wrote a book—"

"Yeah, but it all started back then," he interrupted. "Everything that followed—Wheaton, the book on Job, the Bible study groups—was a grasping attempt to prove wrong what I should have learned from that one phone call. Nobody's out there, Philip. And if by some chance God does exist, then he's toying with us. Why doesn't he quit playing games and show himself?"

3

Richard soon changed the topic of conversation, and we spent the rest of the lunch catching up on the past three years. He kept insisting that he was happy. He may have been protesting too strongly, but he did indeed seem more content.

Toward the end, as we were digging into our ice cream desserts, he brought up our last meeting, three years before. "You must have thought I was half-crazy, charging in there and blurting out my whole life story when I'd never even met you."

"Not at all," I said. "In a strange sort of way, I've never been able to get that conversation out of my mind. Actually, your complaints against God helped me better understand my own."

I then told Richard about the three questions. After I had explained them, I asked if they summed up his complaints against God.

"Well, my doubt was more like a feeling—I felt jilted, like God had strung me along just to watch me fall. But you're right, as

I think about it; those questions were behind my feelings. God was certainly unfair. And he always seemed hidden, and silent. Yeah, that's it. That's it exactly!" he said.

"Why on earth doesn't God answer those questions!" Richard had raised his voice and was waving his arms like a politician— like an evangelist. Fortunately, the restaurant had emptied. "If only God answered those questions—if only he answered *one* of them. If, say, he would just speak aloud one time so that everyone could hear, then I would believe. Probably the whole world would believe. Why doesn't he?"

Chapter 4

What If

"IF ONLY," Richard had said. If only God solved those three problems, then faith would flourish like flowers in springtime. Wouldn't it?

The same year I met Richard in the Mexican restaurant, I happened to be studying the books of Exodus and Numbers. And even though Richard's questions were still buzzing about in my mind, it took a while for me to notice a curious parallel. Then one day it suddenly jumped out from the page: Exodus described the very world Richard wanted! It showed God stepping into human history almost daily. He acted with utter fairness and spoke so that everyone could hear. Behold, he even made himself visible!

The contrast between the days of the Israelites and our days, the twentieth century, got me thinking about how God runs the world, and I went back to the three questions. If God has the power to act fairly, speak audibly, and appear visibly, why, then, does he seem so reluctant to intervene today? Perhaps the record of the Israelites in the wilderness contained a clue.

Question: Is God unfair? Why doesn't he consistently punish evil people and reward good people? Why do awful things happen to people good and bad, with no discernible pattern?

Imagine a world designed so that we experience a mild jolt of pain with every sin and a tickle of pleasure with every act of virtue. Imagine a world in which every errant doctrine attracts a lightning bolt, while every repetition of the Apostles' Creed stimulates our brains to produce an endorphin of pleasure.

The Old Testament records a "behavior modification" experiment almost that blatant: God's covenant with the Israelites. In the Sinai Desert, God resolved to reward and punish his people with strict, legislated fairness. He signed the guarantee with his own hand, making it dependent on the one condition that the Israelites had to follow the laws he laid down. He then had Moses outline the terms of this guarantee to the people:

Results of Obedience	Results of Disobedience
Prosperous cities and rural areas	Violence, crime, and poverty everywhere
No sterility among men, women, or livestock	Infertility among people and livestock
Assured success in farming	Crop failure; locusts and worms
Dependable weather conditions	Scorching heat, drought, blight, and mildew
Guaranteed military victories	Domination by other nations
Total immunity to diseases	Fever and inflammation; madness, blindness, confusion of mind

If they were obedient, Moses said, God would set them "high above all the nations on earth"; they would "always be at the top, never at the bottom." In effect, the Israelites were promised protection from virtually every kind of human misery and disappointment. On the other hand, if they disobeyed they would become "a thing of horror and an object of scorn and ridicule to all the nations where the Lord will drive you. . . . Because you did not serve the Lord your God joyfully and gladly in the time of prosperity, therefore in hunger and thirst, in nakedness and dire poverty, you will serve the enemies the Lord sends against you."

I read on, scanning the books of Joshua and Judges to see the results of this covenant based on a "fair" system of rewards and punishment. Within fifty years the Israelites had disintegrated into a state of utter anarchy. Much of the rest of the Old Testament recounts the dreary history of the predicted curses—not blessings—coming true. Despite all the lavish benefits of the covenant, Israel failed to obey God and meet its terms.

Years later when New Testament authors looked back on that history, they did not hold up the covenant as an exemplary model of God relating to his people with absolute consistency and fairness. Rather, they said the old covenant served as an object lesson, demonstrating that human beings were incapable of fulfilling a contract with God. It seemed clear to them that a new covenant ("testament") with God was needed, one based on forgiveness and grace. And that is precisely why the "New Testament" exists.

Question: Is God silent? If he is so concerned about our doing his will, why doesn't he reveal that will more plainly?

Various people claim to hear the word of God today. Some of them are crazy, like the wild man who on "God's orders" attacked Michelangelo's *Pietà* with a hammer, or the political assassin who claimed God told him to shoot the president. Others seem sincere but misguided, like the six strangers who reported to author Joni Eareckson that God had instructed them to marry her. Still others seem to carry on the authentic tradition of the prophets and apostles, delivering the word of God to his people. So then, how can we know whether what we have heard is truly a word from God?

God simplified matters of guidance, I discovered, when the Israelites camped in the Sinai wilderness. *Should we pack up our tent and move today or stay put?* For the answer, an inquisitive Israelite need only glance at the cloud over the tabernacle. If the cloud moved, God wanted his people to move. If it stayed, that meant stay. (You could conveniently check God's will around the clock; at night the cloud glowed like a tower of fire.)

God set up other ways, like the casting of lots and the Urim and Thummim, to directly communicate his will, but most issues were pre-decided. He had spoken his will for the Israelites in a set of rules, codified into 613 laws that covered the complete range of behavior, from murder to boiling a young goat in its mother's milk. Few people complained about fuzzy guidance in those days.

But did a clear word from God increase the likelihood of obedience? Apparently not. "Do not go up and fight [the Amorites]," said God, "because I will not be with you. You will be defeated by your enemies." The Israelites promptly went up and fought the Amorites and were defeated by their enemies. They marched when told to sit tight, fled in fear when told to march, fought when told to declare peace, declared peace when told to fight. They made a national pastime out of inventing ways to break the 613 commands. Clear guidance became as much of an affront to that generation as unclear guidance is to ours.

I also noticed a telling pattern in the Old Testament accounts: the very clarity of God's will had a stunting effect on the Israelites' faith. Why pursue God when he had already revealed himself so clearly? Why step out in faith when God had already guaranteed the results? Why wrestle with the dilemma of conflicting choices when God had already resolved the dilemma? In short, why should the Israelites act like adults when they could act like children? And act like children they did, grumbling against their leaders, cheating on the strict rules governing manna, whining about every food or water shortage.

As I studied the story of the Israelites, I had second thoughts about crystal-clear guidance. It may serve some purpose—it may, for example, get a mob of just-freed slaves across a hostile desert—but it does not seem to encourage spiritual development. In fact, for the Israelites it nearly eliminated the need for faith at all; clear guidance sucked away freedom, making every choice a matter of obedience rather than faith. And in forty years of wilderness wanderings, the Israelites flunked the obedience test so badly that God was forced to start over with a new generation.

Question: Is God hidden? Why doesn't he simply show up sometime, visibly, and dumbfound the skeptics once and for all?

What the Soviet cosmonaut wanted when he looked for God in the dark void outside his spacecraft window, what my friend Richard wanted, alone in his room at two in the morning, is the hungering desire of our age (for those who still hunger). We want proof, evidence, a personal appearance, so that the God we have heard about becomes the God we see.

What we hunger for happened once. For a time God did show up in person, and a man spoke to him face to face as he might speak with a friend. They met together, God and Moses, in a tent pitched just outside the Israelite camp. The rendezvous was no secret. Whenever Moses trudged over to the tent to talk with God, the whole camp turned out to watch. A pillar of cloud, God's visible presence, blocked the entrance to the tent. No one except Moses knew what transpired inside; no one wanted to know. The Israelites had learned to keep their distance. "Speak to us yourself and we will listen," they said to Moses. "But do not have God speak to us or we will die." After each meeting Moses would emerge glowing like a space alien, and the people turned their faces away until he covered himself with a veil.

There were few, if any, atheists in those days. No Israelites wrote plays about waiting for a God who never arrived. They could see clear evidence of God outside the tent of meeting or in the thick storm clouds hovering around Mount Sinai. A skeptic need only hike over to the trembling mountain and reach out a hand to touch it, and his doubts would vanish—one second before he did.

And yet what happened during those days almost defies belief. When Moses climbed the sacred mountain stormy with the signs of God's presence, those people who had lived through the ten plagues of Egypt, who had crossed the Red Sea on dry ground, who had drunk water from a rock, who were digesting the miracle of manna in their stomachs at that moment—those same people got bored or impatient or rebellious or jealous and apparently forgot all about their God. By the time Moses descended from the mountain, they were dancing like heathens around a golden calf.

God did not play hide-and-seek with the Israelites; they had every proof of his existence you could ask for. But astonishingly— and I could hardly believe this result, even as I read it—God's directness seemed to produce the very *opposite* of the desired effect. The Israelites responded not with worship and love, but

47

with fear and open rebellion. God's visible presence did nothing to improve lasting faith.

3

I had distilled Richard's complaints about God into three questions. But Exodus and Numbers taught me that quick solutions to those three questions may not solve the underlying problems of disappointment with God. The Israelites, though exposed to the bright, unshaded light of God's presence, were as fickle a people as have ever lived. Ten different times on the melancholy pathless plains of the Sinai they rose up against God. Even at the very border of the Promised Land, with all its bounty stretching out before them, they were still keening for the "good old days" of slavery in Egypt.

These dismal results may provide insight into why God does not intervene more directly today. Some Christians long for a world well-stocked with miracles and spectacular signs of God's presence. I hear wistful sermons on the parting of the Red Sea and the ten plagues and the daily manna in the wilderness, as if the speakers yearn for God to unleash his power like that today. But the follow-the-dots journey of the Israelites should give us pause. Would a burst of miracles nourish faith? Not the kind of faith God seems interested in, evidently. The Israelites give ample proof that signs may only addict us to signs, not to God.

True, the Israelites were a primitive people emerging out of slavery. But the biblical accounts have a disturbingly familiar ring to them. The Israelites tended to behave, in Frederick Buechner's phrase, "just like everybody else, only more so."

I came away from my study of them both surprised and confused: surprised to learn how little difference it made in people's lives when three major reasons for disappointment with God—unfairness, silence, and hiddenness—were removed; confused by the questions stirred up about God's actions on earth. Has he changed? Has he pulled back, withdrawn?

As Richard sat in my living room telling me his story that first time, he had looked up suddenly and said in a fierce voice, "God doesn't know what the HELL he's doing with this world!" What is God doing? What is the human experiment all about? What does he want from us, after all, and what can we expect from him?

> *Without somehow destroying me in the process, how could God reveal himself in a way that would leave no room for doubt? If there were no room for doubt, there would be no room for me.*
> —*Frederick Buechner*

Bible references: Deuteronomy 9, 7, 28; Romans 3; Galatians 3; Exodus 28, 40; Deuteronomy 1–2; Exodus 19–20, 32–33; Deuteronomy 1.

Chapter 5

The Source

FOR TWO WEEKS I holed up in a Colorado cabin to ponder Richard's three questions in light of what I had seen in the Old Testament. I brought along a suitcase full of books to study, but during my entire time there I opened only a Bible.

I started at Genesis late the first afternoon, a day of heavy snowfall. It was a perfect setting for reading the story of creation. Clouds lifted in time for a spectacular alpenglow sunset, with puffs of snow pluming off the tops of the mountain peaks, like pink cotton candy. At night the clouds closed in again, and snow blew furiously.

I read straight through the Bible, slowly, cover to cover. By the time I reached Deuteronomy, snow covered the bottom step; when I hit the Prophets it had crept up the mailbox post; and when I finally made it to Revelation I had to call for a snowplow to unbury the driveway. Over seventy-two inches of fresh powder fell during the two weeks I spent in a loft reading the Bible and looking out the window at sugar-coated evergreens.

It struck me forcefully there that our common impressions of God may be very different from the God the Bible actually portrays. What is he really like? In church and at a Christian college I had learned to think of God as an unchanging, invisible spirit who possesses such qualities as omnipotence, omniscience, and impassibility (incapable of emotion). These doctrines, which are supposed to help us understand God's point of view, can be found in the Bible, but they are well buried.

Simply reading the Bible, I encountered not a misty vapor but an actual Person. A Person as unique and distinctive and colorful as any person I know. God has deep emotions; he feels delight and frustration and anger. In the Prophets he weeps and moans with pain, even comparing himself to a woman giving birth: "I cry out, I gasp and pant." Again and again God is shocked by the behavior of human beings. When the Israelites commit infant sacrifice, he seems stunned by actions which—an omniscient God is speaking here—"I did not command or mention, nor did it enter my mind." He explains the need to punish by asking plaintively, "What else can I do?" I know, I know, the word "anthropomorphism" is supposed to explain all those humanlike characteristics. But surely the images God "borrows" from human experience point to an even stronger reality.

As I read through the Bible in my winter aerie, I marveled at how much God lets human beings affect him. I was unprepared for the joy and anguish—in short, the passion—of the God of the Universe. By studying "about" God, by taming him and reducing him to words and concepts that could be filed away in alphabetical order, I had lost the force of the passionate relationship God seeks above all else. The people who related to God best—Abraham, Moses, David, Isaiah, Jeremiah—treated him with startling familiarity. They talked to God as if he were sitting in a chair beside them, as one might talk to a counselor, a boss, a parent, or a lover. They treated him like a person.

That Colorado trip put my three questions about disappointment with God in a new light. They are not puzzles awaiting solution, such as you would encounter in the field of mathematics or computer programming or even philosophy. Rather, they are problems of relationship between human beings and a God who wants desperately to love and be loved by us.

I saw few people during my two-week retreat. Mostly I huddled indoors, behind the wall of snow, and read. Perhaps it was this aloneness, this isolation, that cleared the way for the conclusion that I reached: I had always considered just one point of view, the human point of view. I have shelves full of books presenting the dilemma of being human. Some are funny, some anguished, some sarcastic, some densely philosophical, but all express the same basic viewpoint: "Here's what it feels like to be a human being." People disappointed with God likewise focus on the human point of view. When we ask our questions—Why is God unfair? Silent? Hidden?—we're really asking, Why is God unfair *to me*? Why does he seem silent *with me*, and hidden *from me*?

I tried to set aside my existential questions, my personal disappointments, and consider instead God's point of view. Why does he seek contact with human beings in the first place? What is he pursuing in us, and what interferes with that pursuit? I turned to the Bible again, trying to hear God's words as if for the first time. He speaks for himself there, and I realized that I had not often paid attention. I had been too preoccupied with my feelings to listen attentively to *his* feelings.

I came away from Colorado with a very different mental image of God. After two weeks of studying the Bible, I had a strong sense that God doesn't care so much about being analyzed. Mainly, he wants to be loved. Nearly every page of his Word rustles with this message. And I returned home knowing I must somehow explore the relationship between a passionate God—hungry for the love of his people—and the people themselves. All feelings of disappointment with God trace back to a breakdown in that relationship. Thus, I determined to look for the answer to a question I had never before considered: "What does it feel like to be God?"

The reason the mass of men fear God, and at bottom dislike Him, is because they rather distrust his heart, and fancy Him all brain like a watch.

—Herman Melville

Bible references: Isaiah 42; Jeremiah 19, 9.

Part Two

Making Contact:
The Father

Chapter 6

Risky Business

To understand how it feels to be God, there is only one place to begin: the moment of creation. Often Genesis 1 gets read as a prelude, as our minds speed ahead to the major disruption in chapter 3 or to the modern debate over the process used in creation. But Genesis 1 says nothing of that process or of the tragedy to follow. It lays out the barest sketch of our world—sun and stars, oceans and plants, fish and beasts, man and woman—along with God's own comment on each new work.

"And God saw that it was good"—five times the understatement beats in cadence like a drum. And when he had finished, "God saw all that he had made, and it was very good." Other parts of the Bible recall the time with more exuberance. "The morning stars sang together and all the angels shouted for joy," God reported with pride to Job. Proverbs expands on the upbeat mood: "I was the craftsman at his side. I was filled with delight day after day, rejoicing always in his presence, rejoicing in his whole world and delighting in mankind."

Creation as it felt to God—since then every artist has felt an echo, a sympathetic vibration: a craftsman who squints at his finished product and reckons, "Very good"; a performer who cannot suppress a grin when the audience stands and cheers; even a child with her glued-together Popsicle sticks.

Anthropologist and essayist Loren Eiseley tells of a day when he felt the joy of original creation. An old man then, walking a deserted beach, he found shelter from damp fog under the prow of a wrecked boat and promptly fell asleep. When he opened his eyes, he was looking at the two small neat ears and inquisitive face of a young fox, so young that it had not learned to fear. There, under the boat's shadow, the distinguished naturalist and the fox pup stared at one another. And then the tiny fox, a vast and playful humor in his face, selected a chicken bone from a pile and shook it in his teeth. On impulse Eiseley bent over and grabbed the other end, and the frolic began.

Loren Eiseley: "It has been said repeatedly that one can never, try as he will, get around to the front of the universe. Man is destined to see only its far side, to realize nature only in retreat. Yet here was the thing in the midst of the bones, the wide-eyed innocent fox inviting me to play. The universe was swinging in some fantastic fashion around to present its face, and the face was so small that the universe itself was laughing. It was not a time for human dignity.

"For just a moment I had held the universe at bay by the simple expedient of sitting on my haunches before a fox den and tumbling about with a chicken bone." It was "the gravest, most meaningful act I shall ever accomplish," he later concluded, for in it he had caught at last a glimpse of the universe as it begins for all things. "It was, in reality, a child's universe, a tiny and laughing universe."[1]

Despite the awesome emptiness of our universe, despite the pain that haunts it, something lingers, like a scent of old perfume, from that moment of beginnings in Genesis 1. I too have sensed it. The first time I rounded a bend and saw Yosemite Valley spread out before me, its angel-hair waterfalls spilling over the snow-glazed granite. On a small peninsula of Ontario where five million migrating monarch butterflies stop to rest, their papery wings adorning every tree with shimmering, translucent orange. In the children's zoo in Chicago's Lincoln Park, where every beast born—gorilla, aardvark, or hippopotamus—begins life mischievous and full of play.

Eiseley is right: at the heart of the universe is a smile, a pulse of joy passed down from the moment of creation. A new parent who holds a baby, *my* baby, close against flesh for the first time knows it. And that is the feeling God had when he looked over what he had made and pronounced it good. In the beginning, the very beginning, there was no disappointment. Only joy.

Adam and Eve

Genesis 1 does not tell the whole story of creation, however. To understand what follows, you must create something for yourself.

Every creator, from a child with Play-Doh to Michelangelo, learns that creation involves a kind of self-limiting. You produce something that did not exist before, yes, but only by ruling out other options along the way. Stick the curved clay trunk on the front of the elephant; now it cannot go on the rear or on the side. Pick up a pencil and start drawing; now you limit yourself to black and white, not color.

No artist, no matter how great, escapes this limitation. Michelangelo knew that no *trompe l'oeil* would give the Sistine Chapel ceiling the three-dimensional reality he had achieved in his sculptures. When he decided on a medium, paint on plaster, he limited himself.

When God created, he invented the media as he went, calling into being what had existed only in his imagination, and along with every free choice came a limitation. He chose a world of time and space, a "medium" with peculiar restrictions: first A happens, then B happens, and then C. God, who sees future, past, and present all at once, selected sequential time as an artist selects a canvas and palette, and his choice imposed limits we have lived with ever since. (Hasidic scholars have a wonderful word for God's self-limitation: *zimsum*, they call it.)

"And God said, 'Let the water teem with living creatures.'" Behind that sentence lay a thousand decisions: fish with gills and not lungs, scales not fur, fins not feet, blood not sap. At every stage God the Creator made choices, eliminating alternatives.

Genesis tells of God's final set of choices, then pauses, backs up, and retells it in more detail. On the sixth day of creation, man and woman came into being, two creatures unlike all others. God designed them in his own image, desiring to recognize something of himself in them. They were like a mirror, reflecting back his own likeness.

But Adam and Eve had another distinction as well: alone of all God's creatures, they had a moral capacity to rebel against their creator. The sculptures could spit at the sculptor; the characters in the play could rewrite the lines. They were, in a word, free.

"Man is God's risk," said one theologian. Another, Søren Kierkegaard, put it this way: "God has, so to speak, imprisoned himself in his resolve." Nearly everything theologians say about human freedom sounds somehow right and somehow wrong. How can a sovereign God take risks or imprison himself? Yet God's creation of man and woman approached that kind of astonishing self-limitation.

Consider a rather fanciful rendition of creation by William Irwin Thompson:

> Imagine God in Heaven surrounded by the choirs of adoring angels singing hosannahs unendingly . . . "If I create a perfect world, I know how it will turn out. In its absolute perfection, it will revolve like a perfect machine, never deviating from My absolute will." Since God's imagination is perfect, there is no need for Him to create such a universe: it is enough for Him to imagine it to see it in all its details. Such a universe would not be very interesting to man or God, so we can assume that the Divinity continued His meditations. "But what if I create a universe that is free, free even of me? What if I veil My Divinity so that the creatures are free to pursue their individual lives without being overwhelmed by My overpowering Presence? Will the creatures love Me? Can I be loved by

creatures whom I have not programmed to adore me forever? Can love arise out of freedom? My angels love me unceasingly, but they can see Me at all times. What if I create beings in My own image as a Creator, beings who are free? But if I introduce freedom into this universe, I take the risk of introducing Evil into it as well, for if they are free, then they are free to deviate from My will. Hmmm. But what if I continue to interact with this dynamic universe, what if I and the creatures become the creators together of a great cosmic play? What if out of every occasion of evil, I respond with an unimaginable good, a good that overwhelms evil by springing out of the very attempts of evil to deny the Good? Will these new creatures of freedom then love Me, will they join with Me in creating Good out of Evil, novelty out of freedom? What if I join with them in the world of limitation and form, the world of suffering and evil? Ahh, in a truly free universe, even I do not know how it will turn out. Do even I dare to take that risk for love?"[2]

Why would Adam and Eve want to rebel? They lived in a garden paradise, and if they had a complaint they could talk it over with God as with a friend. But there was that one forbidden tree, the one with the enticing name, "the tree of the knowledge of good and evil." Apparently God was keeping something from them. What secret lay behind that name? And how would they ever know unless they tried? Adam and Eve made their own "creative" choice: they ate the fruit, and earth has never been the same.

Genesis 3 shows exactly what God felt when Adam and Eve disobeyed: sadness over the broken relationship; anger at their denials; and an emotion surprisingly like alarm. "The man has now become like one of us, knowing good and evil. He must not be allowed to reach out his hand and take also from the tree of life and eat, and live forever."

Creation, which seems like pure freedom, involves limitation. And as Adam and Eve soon learned, rebellion, which also seems like freedom, involves limitation as well. By their choice they put distance between themselves and God. Before, they had walked and talked with God. Now when they heard his approach, they hid in the shrubbery. An awkward separation had crept in to spoil the intimacy. And every quiver of disappointment in our own relationship with God is an aftershock from their initial act of rebellion.

> *Perhaps we do not realize the problem, so to call it, of enabling finite free wills to co-exist with Omnipotence. It seems to involve at every moment almost a sort of "divine abdication."*
> —C. S. Lewis

[1] Loren Eiseley, *The Star Thrower*, 64–65.
[2] William I. Thompson, *The Time Falling Bodies Take to Light*, 24–25.

Bible references: Job 38; Proverbs 8; Genesis 1–3.

Chapter 7

The Parent

AFTER MY RETURN from Colorado, I read Genesis over and over, searching the book of beginnings for some clue into what God had in mind for this world. Even after that first landmark rebellion against him, God did not cast off his creation. Genesis tells amazing stories of his continuing personal encounters with humanity.

If I had to reduce the "plot" of Genesis to one sentence, it would be something like this: God learns how to be a parent.* The disruption in Eden changed the world forever, destroying the intimacy Adam and Eve had known with God. In a kind of warm-

---

*A phrase like "God learns" may seem strange because we normally think of learning as a mental process, moving in sequence from a state of not-knowing to a state of knowing. God, of course, is not bound by time or ignorance. He "learns" in the sense of taking on new experiences, such as the creation of free human beings. Using the word in a similar sense, Hebrews says that Jesus "learned obedience from what he suffered."

up to history, God and human beings had to get used to each other. The humans set the pace by breaking all the rules, and God responded with individualized punishments. What did it feel like to be God? What does it feel like to be the parent of a two-year-old?

No one could accuse God of being shy to intervene in the early days. He seemed a close, even hovering parent. When Adam sinned, God met with him in person, explaining that all creation would have to adjust to the choice he, Adam, had made. Just one generation later a new kind of horror—murder—appeared on earth. "What have you done?" God demanded of Cain. "Listen! Your brother's blood cries out to me from the ground." Once again God met with the culprit and custom-designed a punishment.

The state of the earth and, indeed, the entire human race continued to deteriorate toward a point of crisis which the Bible sums up in the most poignant sentence ever written: "The Lord was grieved that he had made man on the earth, and his heart was filled with pain." Behind that one statement stands all the shock and grief God felt as a parent.

What human parent has not experienced at least a pang of such remorse? A teenage son tears away in a fit of rebellion. "I hate you!" he cries, fumbling for words that will cause the most pain. He seems bent on twisting a knife in the belly of his parents. That rejection is what God experienced not just from one child, but from the entire human race. As a result, what God had created, God destroyed. All the joy of Genesis 1 vanished under the churning waters of the Flood.

But there was Noah, that one man of faith who "walked with God." After the remorse expressed in Genesis 3 through 7, you can almost hear God sigh with relief as Noah, in his first act back on land, worships the God who had saved him. *At last, someone to build on.* (Years later, in a message to Ezekiel, God would mention Noah as one of his three most righteous followers.) With the whole planet freshly scrubbed and sprouting life anew, God agreed to a covenant or contract that bound him not just to Noah but to every living creature. It promised one thing only: that God would never again destroy all creation.

The Parent

You could view the covenant with Noah as the barest minimum of a relationship: one party agrees not to obliterate the other. And yet even in that promise God limited himself. He, the sworn enemy of all evil in the universe, pledged to endure wickedness on this planet for a time—or, rather, to solve it through some means other than annihilation. Like the parent of a runaway teenager, he forced himself into the role of The Waiting Father (as Jesus' story of the Prodigal Son expresses so eloquently). Before long another mass rebellion, at a place called Babel, tested God's resolve, and he kept his promise not to destroy.

In earliest history, then, God acted so plainly that no one could grouse about his hiddenness or silence. Yet those early interventions shared one important feature: each was a punishment, a response to human rebellion. If it was God's intention to have a mature relationship with free human beings, he certainly met with a series of rude setbacks. How could he ever relate to his creation as adults when they kept behaving like children?

The Plan

Genesis 12 marks a momentous change. For the first time since the days of Adam, God stepped in not to punish, but to set into motion a new plan for human history.

There was no mystery about what he had in mind. He told Abraham forthrightly: "I will make you into a great nation, with many people bearing your name, and from that nation I will bless all peoples on earth." The plan appears in some form in Genesis 13, 15, 16, and 17 as well as dozens of other Old Testament passages. Rather than trying to restore the whole earth at once, God would begin with a pioneer settlement, a new race set apart from all others. Abraham, dazzled by God's promises, left home and migrated hundreds of miles to the land of Canaan.

Despite the honor accorded him as the father of this new race, however, Abraham emerges as the Bible's first example of a person severely disappointed in God. Miracles, he had. Abraham entertained angels in his home and dreamed mystical visions of smoking fire pots. But there was one nagging problem: after the

65

promise, after the blaze of revelation, came silence—long years of bewildering silence.

"Go, claim the land I have for you," God said. But Abraham found Canaan dry as bone, its inhabitants dying of famine. To stay alive, he fled to Egypt.

"You'll have descendants as countless as the stars in the sky," God said. No promise could have made Abraham happier. At age seventy-five he still anticipated a tent filled with the sounds of children at play. At eighty-five he worked out a backup plan with a female servant. At ninety-nine the promise seemed downright ludicrous, and when God showed up to confirm it, Abraham laughed in his face. A father at ninety-nine? Sarah in maternity clothes at ninety? They both cackled at the thought.

A laugh of ridicule and also of pain. God had dangled a bright dream of fertility before a barren couple and then sat on his hands and watched as they advanced toward tottery old age. What kind of game was he playing? Whatever did he want?

God wanted faith, the Bible says, and that is the lesson Abraham finally learned. He learned to believe when there was no reason left to believe. And although he did not live to see the Hebrews fill the land as the stars fill the sky, Abraham did live to see Sarah bear one child—just one—a boy, who forever preserved the memory of absurd faith, for his name Isaac meant "laughter."

And the pattern continued: Isaac married a barren woman, as did his son Jacob. The esteemed matriarchs of the covenant— Sarah, Rebekah, and Rachel—all spent their best childbearing years slender and in despair. They too experienced the blaze of revelation, followed by dark and lonely times of waiting that nothing but faith would fill.

A gambler would say God stacked the odds against himself. A cynic would say God taunted the creatures he was supposed to love. The Bible simply uses the cryptic phrase "by faith" to describe what they went through. Somehow, that "faith" was what God valued, and it soon became clear that faith was the best way for humans to express a love for God.

Joseph

If you read Genesis in one sitting, you cannot help noticing a change in how God related to his people. At first he stayed close by, walking in the garden with them, punishing their individual sins, speaking to them directly, intervening constantly. Even in Abraham's day he sent extraterrestrial messengers on house calls. By Jacob's time, however, the messages were far more ambiguous: a mysterious dream about a ladder, a late-night wrestling match. And toward the end of Genesis, a man named Joseph received guidance in the most unexpected ways.

Genesis slows down when it gets to Joseph, and it shows God working mostly behind the scenes. God spoke to Joseph not through angels, but through such means as the dreams of a despotic Egyptian pharaoh.

If anyone had a valid reason to be disappointed in God, it was Joseph, whose valiant stabs at goodness brought him nothing but trouble. He interpreted a dream to his brothers, and they threw him in a cistern. He resisted a sexual advance and landed in an Egyptian prison. There, he interpreted another dream to save a cell mate's life, and the cell mate promptly forgot about him. I wonder, as Joseph languished for his virtue in an Egyptian dungeon, did questions like Richard's—Is God unfair? Silent? Hidden?—occur to him?

But shift for a moment to the perspective of God the parent. Had he deliberately "pulled back" to allow Joseph's faith to reach a new level of maturity? And could this be why Genesis devotes more space to Joseph than to any other person? Through all his trials, Joseph learned to trust: not that God would prevent hardship, but that he would redeem even the hardship. Choking back tears, Joseph tried to explain his faith to his murderous brothers: "You intended to harm me, but God intended it for good. . . ."

The central idea of the great part of the Old Testament may be called the idea of the loneliness of God.

—G. K. Chesterton

Bible references: Genesis 1–11; Hebrews 5; Ezekiel 14; Genesis 12–21, 25, 30; Hebrews 11; Genesis 37, 39–41, 45.

Chapter 8

Unfiltered Sunlight

G ENESIS CLOSES with a single family, small enough for the
Bible to name all its sons, settling into the friendly haven
of Egypt. The next book, Exodus, opens with a swarm of Israelites
toiling as slaves under a hostile pharaoh. Nowhere in the Bible
will you find an account of what happened during the intervening
four hundred years.

I have heard many sermons on the life of Joseph, and many
more on Moses and the miracle of the Exodus. But I have never
heard a sermon on the four-hundred-year gap between Genesis
and Exodus. (Could some of our feelings of disappointment stem
from a habit of skipping over times of silence in favor of the
Bible's stories of victory?) We tend to speed ahead to the
exhilarating stories of liberation from slavery. But think of it! For
an ellipsis of time twice as long as the U.S.A. has been in
existence, heaven was silent. Surely the Hebrew slaves in Egypt
felt profound disappointment with God.

You are a Hebrew, a descendant of Abraham. You grew up hearing about the wonderful promises God gave that great man. "Someday your race will become a mighty nation and will live at peace in their own land"—God swore that in person, first to Abraham, and then to Isaac and Jacob. As a child you obediently memorized those promises. But they now seem like fairy tales. Independent nation? You and your neighbors serve the most powerful empire on earth; daily, you suffer the insults and feel the whips of Egyptian taskmasters. Your own infant brother was slaughtered by the pharaoh's soldiers.

As for the vaunted Promised Land, it lies somewhere to the east, divided under the dominion of a dozen kings.

Four hundred years of silence, until Moses, when suddenly anything a skeptic might have wished for happened. First, God appeared in a burning bush, introducing himself to Moses by name. He spoke aloud. "My people have suffered enough," said God. "Now you will see what I will do." Next, he let loose with the most bravura display of divine power the world has ever seen. Ten times he intervened on a scale so massive that not a single person in Egypt could doubt the existence of the God of the Hebrews. Billions of frogs, gnats, flies, hailstones, and locusts gave empirical proof of the Lord of all creation.

For the next forty years, the years of wilderness wanderings, God carried his people "as a father carries his son." He fed the Israelites, clothed them, planned their daily itinerary, and fought their battles.

Is God unfair? Silent? Hidden? Such questions must have troubled the Hebrews until, in Moses' lifetime, God took off the wraps. He punished evil and rewarded good. He spoke audibly. And he made himself visible, first to Moses in a burning bush and then to the Israelites in a pillar of cloud and fire.

The response of the Israelites to such direct intervention

70

offers an important insight into the inherent limits of all power. Power can do everything but the most important thing: it cannot control love. The ten plagues in Exodus show the power of God over a pharaoh. But the ten major rebellions recorded in Numbers show the impotence of power to bring about what God desired most, the love and faithfulness of his people. No pyrotechnic displays of omnipotence could make them trust and follow him.

We do not need the ancient Israelites to teach us this fact. We can see it today in societies where power runs wild. In a concentration camp, as so many witnesses have told us, the guards possess nearly unlimited power. By applying force, they can make you renounce your God, curse your family, work without pay, eat human excrement, kill and then bury your closest friend or even your own mother. All this is within their power. Only one thing is not: they cannot force you to love them.

The fact that love does not operate according to the rules of power may help explain why God sometimes seems shy to use his power. He created us to love him, but his most impressive displays of miracle—the kind we may secretly long for—do nothing to foster that love. As Douglas John Hall has put it, "God's problem is not that God *is not able* to do certain things. God's problem is that God loves. Love complicates the life of God as it complicates every life."[1]

And when his own love is spurned, even the Lord of the Universe feels in some way helpless, like a parent who has lost what he values most. The Bible records a kind of diary of God's tender relationship with the Israelites:

> On the day you were born your cord was not cut, nor were you washed with water to make you clean, nor were you rubbed with salt or wrapped in cloths. No one looked on you with pity or had compassion enough to do any of these things for you. Rather, you were thrown out into the open field, for on the day you were born you were despised.
>
> Then I passed by and saw you kicking about in your blood, and as you lay there in your blood I said to you, "Live!"

I made you grow like a plant of the field. You grew up and developed and became the most beautiful of jewels. Your breasts were formed and your hair grew, you who were naked and bare.

Later I passed by, and when I looked at you and saw that you were old enough for love, I spread the corner of my garment over you and covered your nakedness. I gave you my solemn oath and entered into a covenant with you, declares the Sovereign Lord, and you became mine.

I bathed you with water and washed the blood from you and put ointments on you. I clothed you with an embroidered dress and put leather sandals on you. I dressed you in fine linen and covered you with costly garments. I adorned you with jewelry: I put bracelets on your arms and a necklace around your neck, and I put a ring on your nose, earrings on your ears and a beautiful crown on your head.

Yet God, all-seeing, knew the ultimate, tragic destiny of the Israelites: "I know what they are disposed to do, even before I bring them into the land," he said. As his people gathered beside the Jordan River, in an upbeat mood for a change, God allowed a remarkable glimpse into what it feels like to be God. He did not share the spirit of anticipation in the camp, and he visited Moses in the Tent of Meeting to explain why.

More than anything, God longed for the covenant to succeed: "Oh, that their hearts would be inclined to fear me and keep all my commands always, so that it might go well with them and their children forever!" But the repeated rebellions in the wilderness had taken a toll. God predicted a terrible disobedience to come and foretold his own response: "I will certainly hide my face on that day." He spoke with rueful resignation, like the parent of a drug addict, helpless to stop his own child from self-destructing; like the husband of an alcoholic who hears a blubbering promise to do better tomorrow or the next day, a promise his wife has already broken too many times to mention.

Then God gave Moses a very odd assignment. "Write down a song," he said, "and make the Israelites learn it as a witness to history." The song set God's point of view to music: the lament of a lover grieved to the point of desertion. Thus at the birth of their nation, euphoric over the crossing of the Jordan River, the Israelites premiered a kind of national anthem—the strangest that has ever been sung. It had virtually no words of hope, only doom.

They sang first of the favored times, when God found them in a howling wasteland and treasured them as the apple of his eye. They sang of the awful betrayal to come, when they would forget the God who gave them birth. They sang of the curses that would afflict them, the wasting famine, deadly plague, and arrows drunk with blood. With this bittersweet music ringing in their ears, the Israelites marched into the Promised Land.

Like a bloodhound on a trail, I keep zigzagging back to the wanderings in the wilderness to poke around for clues. The tabernacle luminous with God's presence, the miraculous breakfast food, the throng of unhappy Israelites shuffling along in the desert sand—somewhere between the bright promise and the blighted futility of those forty years lies the mystery of disappointment with God. What went wrong?

I have often longed for God to act in a direct, closeup manner. If only he would show himself! But in the Israelites' dreary stories of failure I can perceive certain "disadvantages" to God acting so directly. One problem they encountered immediately was the lack of personal freedom. For the Israelites to live in proximity to a holy God, nothing—not sex, menstruation, the content of clothing fabric, or dietary habits—could fall outside the purview of his laws. Being a "chosen people" had a cost. Just as God found it nearly impossible to live among sinful people, the Israelites found it nearly impossible to live with a holy God in their midst.

Petty things seemed to bother the Israelites most—witness their constant complaints about food. With a few exceptions, they ate the same thing every day for forty years: *manna* (meaning, literally, "What is it?") that appeared like dew on the ground each morning. A monotonous diet may seem a trivial exchange for liberation from slavery, but listen to the grumbling: "We remember the fish we ate in Egypt at no cost—also the cucumbers, melons, leeks, onions and garlic. But now we have lost our appetite; we never see anything but this manna!"

In addition to these mundane issues, a far more serious problem arose. The closer God drew toward his people, paradoxically, the more distant they felt from him. Moses laid down an amazing elaboration of rituals necessary to approach God, and no margin for error. The Israelites could see clear evidence of God's presence in the Most Holy Place—but no one dared enter. If you want to know what kind of "personal relationship with God" the Israelites enjoyed, listen to the words of the worshipers themselves: "We will die! We are lost, we are all lost! Anyone who even comes near the tabernacle of the Lord will die." And again, "Let us not hear the voice of the Lord our God nor see this great fire anymore, or we will die."

Once, as an experiment, the great scientist Isaac Newton stared at the image of the sun reflected in a mirror. The brightness burned into his retina, and he suffered temporary blindness. Even after he hid for three days behind closed shutters, still the bright spot would not fade from his vision. "I used all means to divert my imagination from the sun," he writes, "but if I thought upon him I presently saw his picture though I was in the dark." If he had stared a few minutes longer, Newton might have permanently lost all vision. The chemical receptors that govern eyesight cannot withstand the full force of unfiltered sunlight.

There is a parable in Isaac Newton's experiment, and it helps illustrate what the Israelites ultimately learned from the wilderness wanderings. They had attempted to live with the Lord of the Universe visibly present in their midst; but, in the end, out of all the thousands who had so gladly fled Egypt, only two survived God's Presence. If you can barely endure candlelight, how can you gaze at the sun?

"Who of us can dwell with the consuming fire?" asked the prophet Isaiah. Is it possible that we should be grateful for God's hiddenness, rather than disappointed?

[1]Douglas John Hall, *God and Human Suffering*, 156.

Bible references: Exodus 1–12; Deuteronomy 1; Ezekiel 16; Deuteronomy 31, 5, 31–32; Numbers 11, 17; Deuteronomy 18; Isaiah 33.

Chapter 9

One Shining Moment

NINE-YEAR-OLD Leo Tolstoy, convinced God would help him fly, dove headfirst out a third-floor window and had his first major crisis of disappointment with God. Fortunately, Tolstoy survived the crash landing and, years later, could laugh at his childish test of faith.

What child has not fantasized about supernatural powers? *Lord, help me walk across this lake. Help me beat up that bully. Make me smart without having to study.* And if God ever saw fit to answer some of those prayers, if, like a genie in a bottle, he granted us any wish we wanted, wouldn't we then try to please him out of gratitude? In my dark hours of disappointment, I instinctively think like that: *If God can get me out . . . if things calm down . . . if I get well . . . then I'll follow God.*

My friend Richard believed that anyone would, like a faithful puppy, follow a God who acted fairly, spoke clearly, and made himself obvious. The wilderness wanderings of the Israelites prove him wrong. But, some might argue, their faith faltered in a harsh land, a place remembered by Moses as a "vast and dreadful desert, that thirsty and waterless land, with its venomous snakes and scorpions." Who wouldn't lose heart in those circumstances. Were there happier times, when God seemed close *and* granted his people their desires?

The tone of the Old Testament brightens when the name David shows up. "Then the Lord awoke as from sleep, as a man wakes from the stupor of wine," Psalm 78 says about those days. God had at last found a man after his own heart, the kind of person he could build a nation around. Lusty King David broke every law on the books save one: he loved God with all his heart, all his mind, and all his soul. With David installed as king over Israel, dreams of the covenant came surging back.

And when David's son Solomon took the throne, God pulled out all the stops. What children only dream of, Solomon got. God offered him any wish—long life, riches, anything at all—and when Solomon chose wisdom God added bonus gifts of wealth, honor, and peace. He would rule over a Golden Age, a shining moment of tranquillity in the long, tormented history of the Hebrews.

Solomon

He took over the throne of Israel as a teenager and soon became the richest person of his time. The Bible says that silver was as common in Jerusalem as stones. A fleet of trading ships sought out exotica for the king's private collections—apes and baboons from Africa—and ivory and gold by the ton. Solomon had artistic talent as well: he wrote 1005 songs and 3000 proverbs.

Rulers traveled hundreds of miles to test Solomon's wisdom firsthand and to see the great city he had built. One such ruler, the queen of Sheba, said to him:

> The report I heard in my own country about your achievements and your wisdom is true. But I did not believe these things until I came and saw with my own eyes. Indeed, not even half was told me; in wisdom and wealth you have far

exceeded the report I heard. How happy your men must be! How happy your officials, who continually stand before you and hear your wisdom! Praise be to the Lord your God, who has delighted in you and placed you on the throne of Israel.

Impressive words from a queen who, as a farewell gift, gave Solomon four and a half tons of pure gold.

And what did God feel during these halcyon days? Relief, pleasure, delight—the Bible hints at all these. Israel's chronic grumblers had died off, and Solomon went out of his way to make God feel loved. He lavished the wealth of his kingdom on a tremendous temple, fashioned by 200,000 workmen, that ranked as one of the wonders of the world. From a distance, it shone like a snowcapped mountain.

Old Testament history reached a high-water mark on the day Solomon dedicated that temple to God. Think of a movie scene of the most blinding encounter with an extraterrestrial being. Something like that happened in Jerusalem, only this was no illusion staged by special-effects crews. Thousands of people were looking on in a huge public ceremony. When the glory of the Lord came down to fill the temple, even the priests were driven back by the blast.

God was making Solomon's temple the center of his activity on earth, and the crowd spontaneously decided to stay another two weeks to celebrate. Kneeling on a bronze platform, Solomon prayed aloud, "I have indeed built a magnificent temple for you, a place for you to dwell forever." Then he caught himself in astonishment. "But will God really dwell on earth? The heavens, even the highest heaven, cannot contain you. How much less this temple I have built!"

Later, God responded: "I have heard the prayer and plea you have made before me; I have consecrated this temple. . . . My eyes and my heart will always be there." God had done it! His promises to Abraham and Moses had finally come true. The Israelites now had land, a nation with secure boundaries, and a gleaming symbol of God's presence among them. No one present on the famous day of the temple dedication could doubt God;

everyone saw the fire and the cloud of his presence. And all this came to pass not in a harsh desert full of snakes and scorpions, but in a land rich with silver and gold.

3

With everything imaginable working in his favor, at first it seemed Solomon would gratefully follow God. His prayer of dedication for the temple in 1 Kings 8 is one of the most majestic ever prayed. Yet by the end of his reign Solomon had squandered away nearly every advantage. The poetic man who had sung of romantic love broke all records for promiscuity: seven hundred wives in all, and three hundred concubines! The wise man who had composed so many commonsense proverbs flouted them with an extravagance that has never been equaled. And to please his foreign-born wives, the devout man who had built the temple of God took a final, terrible step: he introduced idol worship into God's holy city.

In one generation, Solomon took Israel from a fledgling kingdom dependent on God for bare survival to a self-sufficient political power. But along the way he lost sight of the original vision to which God had called them. Ironically, by the time of Solomon's death, Israel resembled the Egypt they had escaped: an imperial state held in place by a bloated bureaucracy and slave labor, with an official state religion under the ruler's command. Success in the kingdom of this world had crowded out interest in the kingdom of God. The brief, shining vision of a covenant nation faded away, and God withdrew his sanction. After Solomon's death, Israel split in two and slid toward ruin.

A quotation from Oscar Wilde might provide the best epitaph for Solomon: "In this world there are only two tragedies. One is not getting what one wants, and the other is getting it." Solomon got whatever he wanted, especially when it came to symbols of power and status. Gradually, he depended less on God and more on the props around him: the world's largest harem, a house twice the size of the temple, an army well-stocked with chariots, a strong economy. Success may have eliminated any crises of disappointment with God, but it also seemed to eliminate Solomon's desire for God at all. The more he enjoyed the world's good gifts, the less he thought about the Giver.

In the wilderness God dwelt in a pillar of fire and cloud, so nearby that his power sometimes "broke out" with destructive force. In Solomon's day God seemed to restrict that power, giving the king authority to represent him to the people. As for the Israelites, who had shrunk in fear from God in the wilderness, they simply took God for granted once his presence was centered in the temple. He became just another part of the royal landscape.

In response to this change, God quietly turned elsewhere. You can easily detect the shift by scanning the Old Testament, which gives lengthy accounts of the first three kings of Israel— Saul, David, and Solomon; but after Solomon, stories of the kings speed up into a forgettable blur. God turned instead to his prophets.

Bible references: Deuteronomy 8; 2 Samuel 7; 1 Kings 8–10.

Chapter 10

Fire and the Word

It was an unholy coincidence that many took to be divine retribution. Two weeks ago, canon David Jenkins, 59, who had publicly asserted that neither the Virgin birth nor the Resurrection need be taken too literally, was formally consecrated as Bishop of Durham in York Minster amid cries of protest. Less than three days later, in the early hours of the morning, lightning forked down on the wooden roof of the minster's 13th century south transept. By 2:30 A.M., flames were leaping from the medieval masterpiece that is the largest Gothic cathedral in Northern Europe. . . . Jenkins' detractors lost no time in claiming that their views had been vindicated. . . . a vicar who had been evicted from the minster for voicing protests in the midst of the new bishop's consecration ceremony suggested that "divine intervention" might have caused the fire. Others . . . cit[ed] the prophet Elijah, who brought down a fire from heaven, which destroyed an altar he had built in the presence of the prophets of Baal.

—*Time*, July 23, 1984

The problem with the York Minster lightning bolt, of course, is that it stands as such an exception. So fire from the heavens hits a famous church—what about all the Unitarian churches that brashly deny orthodox Christian doctrines, not to mention the Muslim mosques and Hindu temples? Why should David Jenkins provoke divine wrath when the outright blasphemer Bertrand Russell lived unpunished into cranky old age? If God consistently sent lightning bolts in response to bad doctrine, our planet would sparkle nightly like a Christmas tree.

And yet fire did fall from heaven once, almost thirty centuries ago, and ministers ever since have harked back to that scene on Mount Carmel. The story has a mythic, Tolkienesque quality to it: like Frodo on his mission to Mordor, Elijah journeyed across Israel to a rugged desert mountain to wage war, single-combat style, against 850 false prophets.

Elijah, the wildest and woolliest prophet of Israel, worked the crowd like a master magician. He doused the site with twelve large jars of water—a most precious commodity after three years of drought. And just when it seemed Elijah was perpetrating a huge national joke, it happened. A ball of fire dropped like a meteor from a clear sky. The heat was so intense it melted the stones and soil, and flames lapped up water from the trenches like fuel. The crowd dropped to the ground in fear and awe. "The Lord—he is God! The Lord—he is God!" they cried.

In a dramatic public showdown, God clobbered the forces of evil. No wonder the scene looms large in the annals of faith. No wonder the people of Jesus' day mistook him for Elijah reincarnate. Even in modern times, when lightning strikes a cathedral, some wistfully recall Mount Carmel.

Yet when I sat in a Colorado cabin and read straight through the Bible, I saw the life of Elijah in a very different light. He and his miracle-working twin Elisha emerged not as prototypes of the Old Testament prophet, but as stellar exceptions: few successors had even a trace of their ability to work miracles. If we yearn for their power, we yearn for the wrong thing. The signs and wonders of Elijah's day were a blip in history, with no long-term effect on the Israelites. No wildfire revivals broke out, and after the briefest flurry of religious fervor, the nation settled back into its long, steady slide away from God. King Ahab, himself a spectator at Mount Carmel, left a legacy as Israel's wickedest king.

Apparently the fireball on Mount Carmel had no lasting impact on Elijah either. Terrified for his life, the prophet put forty days' distance between himself and Queen Jezebel, Ahab's vengeful consort. And when God next met with Elijah, he did not appear in a fire, or in a great and powerful wind, or in an earthquake. Rather, he came in a whisper, a thin, small voice almost like silence—a preview of a striking change to come.

The Prophets

It must have been hard to follow the prophet Elijah. Not long after the showdown on Mount Carmel another prophet, Micaiah, stood before the same king, Ahab, in very similar circumstances. Elijah-like, he faced down four hundred false prophets and delivered a stinging message from God. But instead of fire falling from heaven, Micaiah got a slap in the face and a stint in jail.

After Elijah and Elisha, God seemed to rein in his supernatural power, turning from spectacle to word. Most prophets—Isaiah, Hosea, Habakkuk, Jeremiah, Ezekiel—had no stunning displays of omnipotence to dangle before an audience; they had only the power of words. And as God seemed to draw farther and farther away, these prophets themselves began to ask questions: eloquent questions, haunting questions, questions wrapped in pain. They voiced aloud the cries of a people who felt abandoned by God.

I had always misread the prophets—when I bothered to read them at all. I had seen them as finger-wagging, fusty old men who, like Elijah, called down judgment on the pagans. I discovered to my surprise that the ancient prophets' writings actually sound the most "modern" of any part of the Bible. They deal with the very same themes that hang like a cloud over our century: the silence of God, the seeming sovereignty of evil, the unrelieved suffering in the world. The prophets' questions are, in fact, the questions of this book: God's unfairness, silence, hiddenness.

More passionately than anyone in history, the prophets of

Israel gave voice to the feeling of disappointment with God. Why do godless nations flourish? they asked. Why is there such poverty and depravity in the world? Why so few miracles? Where are you, God? "Why do you always forget us? Why do you forsake us so long?" Show yourself; break your silence. For God's sake, literally, ACT!

There was the urbane voice of Isaiah, an aristocrat and adviser to kings, in personal style as far removed from Elijah as Winston Churchill was from Gandhi. "Truly you are a God who hides himself," Isaiah said. "Oh, that you would rend the heavens and come down, that the mountains would tremble before you!"

Jeremiah loudly protested the failure of "success theology." In his day, prophets were being tossed in dungeons and wells, and even sawed in half. Jeremiah compared God to a weakling, "a man taken by surprise . . . a warrior powerless to save." Voltaire himself could not have put it better: How can an all-powerful and all-loving God permit such a messed-up world?

Habakkuk challenged God to explain why, as he put it, "justice never prevails."

> How long, O Lord, must I call for help,
>   but you do not listen?
> Or cry out to you, "Violence!"
>   but you do not save?
> Why do you make me look at injustice?
>   Why do you tolerate wrong?

Like all Israelites, the prophets had been raised on victory stories. As children they had learned how God freed his people from slavery, descended to live among them, and carried them into the Promised Land. But now in visions of the future they saw, in slow-motion detail, all those victories being undone. In a stark reversal of the unforgettable scene from Solomon's day, the prophet Ezekiel watched God's glory rise, hover above the temple for a moment, and then vanish.

What Ezekiel saw in a vision, Jeremiah saw in stark reality. Babylonian soldiers entered the temple—pagans in the Most Holy Place!—looted it, then burned it to the ground. (Historians record that as they entered the temple the soldiers swept the empty air with their spears, seeking the unseen Hebrew God.) Jeremiah wandered the deserted streets of Jerusalem in a state of shock, like a survivor of Hiroshima staggering through the rubble. Israel's king was now shackled and blinded, the nation's princes slaughtered. In the final siege, Jerusalem's gentle women had cooked and eaten their own children.

How did it feel to be a prophet then? Jeremiah tells us:

> Since my people are crushed, I am crushed;
>   I mourn, and horror grips me. . . .
> Oh, that my head were a spring of water
>   and my eyes a fountain of tears!
> I would weep day and night
>   for the slain of my people. . . .
> My heart is broken within me;
>   all my bones tremble.
> I am like a drunken man,
>   like a man overcome by wine.

But the most amazing feature of the prophets is not their "modern" outlook or their passionate cry of disappointment. The reason these seventeen books merit a close look is that they include God's own reply to the prophets' bracing questions.

Bible references: 1 Kings 17-19, 22; Lamentations 5; Isaiah 45, 64; Jeremiah 14; Habakkuk 1; Jeremiah 8-9, 23.

Chapter 11

Wounded Lover

GOD TALKED BACK, defending the way he ran the world. He lashed out, stormed, and wept. And this is what he said: *I am not silent; I have been speaking through my prophets.*

We tend to rank God's revelations by their dramatic effect, with spectacular personal appearances at the top, supernatural miracles just below, and the words of the prophets at the bottom. The fireball on Mount Carmel, for example, seems more convincing than one of Jeremiah's doleful sermons. But God acknowledged no such rating. In an ironic twist, he pointed to the prophets themselves—the very people who were questioning his silence—as proof of his concern. How can a nation complain about the silence of God when they have the likes of Ezekiel and Jeremiah and Daniel and Isaiah?

God did not consider "mere words" an inferior form of proof. Miracles, after all, had never had much lasting impact on the Israelites' faith; but the prophets would inscribe a permanent record, to be passed down over generations, of God's overtures toward his people. Sometimes God pointed to past miracles as proofs of his love, but more often he said something like this, in the familiar tone of an exasperated parent: "From the time your forefathers left Egypt until now, day after day, again and again I sent you my servants the prophets. But they did not listen to me or pay attention." God concluded that the people did not really want a word from the Lord, and they proved him right, warning Isaiah, "Tell us pleasant things, prophesy illusions . . . and stop confronting us with the Holy One of Israel."

I have indeed withdrawn my presence.

When the prophets complained loudly about God's hiddenness, God didn't argue. He agreed with them, and then explained why he was keeping his distance.

To Jeremiah, God expressed his disgust with what he saw in Israel: dishonest gain, the shedding of innocent blood, oppression, extortion. He covered his eyes, he said, refusing even to see hands spread out in a posture of prayer, for those hands were covered with blood.

To Ezekiel, God explained that once Israel's rebellions had passed a certain point, he simply "gave them over" to their sins. He withdrew, letting the people choose their own way and bear the consequences.

To Zechariah, he said, "When I called, they did not listen; so when they called, I would not listen."

My slowness to act is a sign of mercy, not of weakness.

When God did not punish quickly, the people of Israel presumed he had lost his power: "He will do nothing! No harm will come to us; we will never see sword or famine." They were wrong. God's restraint marked an interlude of mercy, a time of probation he was granting Israel. Reluctantly, like a parent out of options, God resorted to punishment.

For Israel, punishment took the form of foreign invasions. But the prophets also speak of a "day of the Lord" at the end of time. Sandwiched between their shining accounts of a new heaven and new earth are some of the most dreadful apocalyptic visions ever set to words. Before we can hear the last word, said Dietrich Bonhoeffer, we must listen to the next-to-the-last word. And the more I study the prophets' accounts of the last days, the more content I become with God's apparent "shyness" to intervene in human affairs.

In my own times of disappointment with God, I have called on him to act with power. I have prayed against political tyranny and unfairness and injustice. I have prayed for miracle, for proof of God's existence. But as I read the prophets' descriptions of the day when God finally will take off all the wraps, one prayer overwhelms all others: "God, I hope I'm not around then." God freely admits he is holding back his power, but he restrains himself for our benefit. For all scoffers who call for direct action from the heavens, the prophets have ominous advice: Just wait.

Though my judgments appear stern, I am suffering with you.

God exposed his deepest feelings to the prophets. For example, here is how he felt about the destruction of Moab, one of Israel's enemies:

> I wail over Moab,
>   for all Moab I cry out. . . .
> My heart laments for Moab like a flute.

As for his chosen people of Israel, whatever shame and humiliation they endured, God also endured. The Israelites watched in horror as Babylonian axmen hacked apart the cedar beams of the temple—but it was God's own house they were invading, and he felt that invasion as a personal desecration. As the temple was razed, his dwelling place was razed. As the Jews were led captive, he was led captive. And when the conquerors divided the spoils of Israel, they joked not about the Israelites but about their weakling God. "Wherever they went among the nations they profaned my holy name, for it was said of them, 'These are the Lord's people, and yet they had to leave his land.'"

A single, elegant sentence from Isaiah summarizes God's point of view: "In all their distress he too was distressed." God may have hidden his face, but that face was streaked with tears.

Despite everything, I am ready to forgive at any moment.

Often, in the midst of a stern reproof, God would stop—literally midsentence—and beg Israel to repent. Ahab, the most wicked king of Israel, got another chance after Mount Carmel, and then another, and another. "I take no pleasure in the death of the wicked," God explained to Ezekiel. "Turn! Turn from your evil ways! Why will you die, O house of Israel?" He told Jeremiah that if he could find just one honest person in Jerusalem, he would spare the whole city.

Nothing expresses God's yearning to forgive better than the Book of Jonah. It contains but one line of prophecy: "Forty more days and Nineveh will be overturned." But, to Jonah's disgust, that simple announcement of doom sparked a spiritual revival in hated Nineveh and changed God's plans for punishment. Jonah, sulking under a shriveled vine, admitted he had suspected God's soft heart all along. "I knew that you are a gracious and compassionate God, slow to anger and abounding in love, a God who relents from sending calamity." Thus the whole madcap scenario of balky prophet, ocean storm, and whale detour came about because Jonah could not trust God—could not, that is, trust him to be harsh and unrelenting toward Nineveh. As Robert Frost summed up the story, "After Jonah, you could never trust God not to be merciful again."

Passion

Although God answered the prophets' questions directly, his explanations did not satisfy Israel. Knowing the reason behind a disaster does not lessen the sense of pain and betrayal. And in truth God's rational "defense" seems tossed in almost as an aside. The prophets are not as concerned about intellectual questions as they are about God's *passion*. How does it feel to be God? To understand, consider the human images stressed again and again by the prophets: God as parent, and as lover.

Follow around some first-time parents. Their conversation seems limited to one topic: The Child. They crow that their wrinkled, ruddy baby is the most beautiful child ever born. They spend hundreds of dollars on equipment to videotape the first babbling words and the first lurching steps—ordinary skills mastered by almost all five billion people on earth. Such strange behavior expresses a new parent's pride and joy in a human relationship like no other.

In choosing Israel, God was seeking such a relationship. He wanted what any parent wants: a happy household of children who return their parent's love. His voice sings with pride as he reminisces about the early days: "Is not Ephraim my dear son, the child in whom I delight?" But the joy fades away as God abruptly shifts from the perspective of a parent to that of a lover, a wounded lover. *What have I done wrong?* he demands in a tone of sadness, and horror, and rage.

> I supplied all their needs,
>   yet they committed adultery
>   and thronged to the houses of prostitutes.
> They are well-fed, lusty stallions,
>   each neighing for another man's wife.
> Should I not punish them for this?

In reading the prophets I cannot help envisioning a counselor with God as a client. The counselor gets out one stock sentence, "Tell me how you really feel," and then God takes over.

"I'll tell you how I feel! I feel like a rejected parent. I find a baby girl lying in a ditch, near death. I take her home and make her my daughter. I clean her, pay for her schooling, feed her. I dote on her, clothe her, hang jewelry on her. Then one day she runs away. I hear reports of her debased life. When my name comes up, she curses me.

"I'll tell you how I feel! I feel like a jilted lover. I found my lover thin and wasted, abused, but I brought her home and made her beauty shine. She is my precious one, the most beautiful woman in the world to me, and I lavish on her gifts and love. And yet she forsakes me. She pants after my best friends, my enemies—anyone. She stands by a highway and under every spreading tree and, worse than a prostitute, she pays people to have sex with her. I feel betrayed, abandoned, cuckolded."

God does not hide his hurt. He employs shocking language, comparing Israel to "a swift she-camel running here and there, a wild donkey accustomed to the desert, sniffing the wind in her craving—in her heat who can restrain her?"

As if words alone were too weak to convey his passion, God asked one brave prophet, Hosea, to act out a living parable. On God's orders, Hosea married Gomer, a woman with a most unsavory reputation. From then on, the poor man lived a soap-opera existence. Time after time Gomer wandered off, fell for another man, and moved out. And each time, incredibly, God instructed Hosea to welcome Gomer back and forgive her.

God used Hosea's unhappy story to illustrate his own whipsaw emotions. That first blush of love when he found Israel, God said, was like finding grapes in the desert. But as Israel broke his trust again and again, he was forced to endure the awful shame of a wounded lover. His words carry a tone not far from self-pity: "I am like a moth to Ephraim, like rot to the people of Judah."

The powerful image of a jilted lover explains why, in his speeches to the prophets, God seems to "change his mind" every few seconds. He is preparing to obliterate Israel—wait, now he is weeping, holding out open arms—no, he is sternly pronouncing judgment again. Those shifting moods seem hopelessly irrational, except to anyone who has been jilted by a lover.

The words of the prophets sound like the words of a lovers' quarrel drifting through thin apartment walls. A neighbor of mine endured two years of such conflict. In November she was ready to kill her unfaithful husband. In February she forgave him and invited him back in. In April she filed for divorce. In August she stopped the proceedings and asked her husband to return again. It took two years for her to face the ugly truth that her love had been rejected forever.

And that is the precise cycle of anger, grief, forgiveness, jealousy, love, pain that God himself went through. The prophets show God struggling for a language, any language, that might break through to his people. Just as my neighbor would hang up the phone on her estranged husband, God would tell the prophets that he would no longer listen to the prayers of Israel. And just as my friend would soften, God would soften and beg his people to try again. Sometimes his love and anger seemed to collide. But at last, all alternatives exhausted, God concluded that he must give up: "What else can I do because of the sin of my people?"

My friend Richard described to me his deep sense of betrayal when God "let him down." He felt exactly as he had when his fiancee abruptly cut him off. But the prophets, and especially Hosea, communicate one message above all others: God is the betrayed one. It was Israel, not God, who had gone a-whoring. The prophets of Israel had expressed a profound disappointment in God, accusing him of acting aloof, unconcerned, silent. But when God spoke, he poured out emotions pent up for centuries. And he, not Israel, was the truly disappointed party.

"What else can I do?" God's poignant question to Jeremiah points up the dilemma of an omnipotent God who has made room for freedom. The stork in the sky knows her seasons, the ocean tide rolls in on schedule, snow always covers the high mountains, but human beings are like nothing else in nature. God cannot control them. Yet he cannot simply thrust them aside either. He cannot get humanity out of his mind.

Bible references: Jeremiah 7; Isaiah 30; Jeremiah 5; Ezekiel 20; Zechariah 7; Jeremiah 5, 48; Ezekiel 36; Isaiah 63; Ezekiel 33; Jonah 3–4; Jeremiah 31, 5, 2; Hosea 9, 5; Jeremiah 9.

Chapter 12

Too Good To Be True

Grief melts away
Like snow in May,
As if there were no such cold thing.
　　　　　　—George Herbert, "The Flower"

ONE DAY when George MacDonald, the great Scottish preacher and writer, was talking with his son, the conversation turned to heaven and the prophets' version of the end of all things. "It seems too good to be true," the son said at one point. A smile crossed MacDonald's whiskered face. "Nay," he replied, "it is just so good it must be true!"[1]

Does any human emotion run as deep as hope? Fairy tales pass on through the centuries a stubborn hope in a happy ending, a belief that in the end the wicked witch will die and the brave and innocent children will somehow find a way of escape. A dozen cartoons in a row on Saturday morning television crank out a similar message to children who sit enthralled, too young to sneer at impossibly cheery endings. In real life, a mother caught in a war zone holds her infant son tight against her breast, pats his head, and whispers, illogically, "It'll be all right," even as the percussive blasts grow closer.

Where does such hope come from? Searching for words to explain the ageless attraction of fairy tales, Tolkien said:

> [Fairy tale] does not deny the existence of . . . sorrow and failure: the possibility of these is necessary to the joy of the deliverance; it denies (in the face of much evidence, if you will) universal final defeat . . . giving a fleeting glimpse of Joy, Joy beyond the walls of the world, poignant as grief.[2]

No summary of the prophets would be complete apart from one last message: their loud insistence that the world will not end in "universal final defeat," but in Joy. They spoke in foreboding times to audiences filled with fear, and often their dire predictions of droughts and locust plagues and enemy sieges fueled that fear. But always, in every one of their seventeen books, the prophets of the Old Testament got around to a word of hope. The wounded lover will recover from his pain, Isaiah promises: "For a brief moment I abandoned you, but with deep compassion I will bring you back."

Their voices soar like songbirds' when the prophets turn at last to describe the Joy beyond the walls of the world. In that final day, God will roll up the earth like a carpet and weave it anew. Wolves and lambs will feed together in the same field, and a lion graze in peace beside an ox.

One day, says Malachi, we will leap like calves released from the stall. There will be no fear then, and no pain. No infants will die; no tears will fall. Among the nations, peace will flow like a river, and armies will melt their weapons into farm tools. No one will complain about the hiddenness of God in that day. His glory will fill the earth, and the sun will seem dim by contrast.

For the prophets, human history is not an end in itself but a transition time, a parenthesis between Eden and the new heaven and new earth still to be formed by God. Even when everything seems out of control, God is firmly in control, and someday will assert himself.*

The Meantime

But what about right now? Must we wait past death for all meaningful answers to the problem of disappointment with God? After the prophets had died off, the Jewish people began to raise such questions, for once again the heavens went silent: "We are given no miraculous signs; no prophets are left, and none of us knows how long this will be. How long will the enemy mock you, O God?"

Torn from their homeland and sold once more into bondage, the Jews hung onto the prophets' promises of a deliverer and a peaceful future. As the decades, even centuries passed, empires—Babylon, Persia, Egypt, Greece, Syria, Rome—rose and fell, their armies chasing each other across the plains of Palestine. Each new empire subjugated the Jews with ease, as if scraping their feet on a doormat. Sometimes the entire race verged on extinction.

No Moses figure appeared to lead the Jews out of bondage. No Elijahs called down fireballs from heaven. No luminous glow radiated from the temple in Jerusalem. Until King Herod came along with his penchant for ostentatious buildings, the temple site remained half-finished, a pile of rubble recalling more shame than glory.

---

*Some people find no comfort in the prophets' vision of a future world. "Mere pie in the sky," they say. "The church has used that line for centuries to justify slavery, oppression, and all manner of injustice. They force-feed the hope of heaven to the poor in order to keep them from demanding too much on earth." The criticism sticks because the church has abused the prophets' vision. But you will never find that "pie in the sky" rationale in the prophets themselves. Amos, Hosea, Isaiah, and Jeremiah have scathing words about the need to care for widows and orphans and aliens, and to clean up corrupt courts and religious systems. The people of God are not merely to mark time, waiting for God to step in and set right all that is wrong. Rather, they are to model the new heaven and new earth, and by so doing awaken longings for what God will someday bring to pass.

At the end of the Old Testament, God was in hiding. He had threatened to hide his face, and when he finally did a dark shadow fell across the planet. Our disappointment with God twenty-five centuries later is a faint aftershock of what the Jews felt when God turned his back. Today, we may find some comfort in looking back on lessons from the past. We may see the "disadvantages" to God's closeup interventions: his Presence, too bright for us, leaves scorch marks; it creates distance; and worse, it doesn't even seem to foster faith. We may also find comfort in looking ahead to eternal life free of tears and pain, in a new dimension somewhere, after we're transformed into beings who can endure God's Presence. But what of the meantime? The mean times? Like the Jews, we feel God's hiddenness as a disappointment, an aching in the heart, a doubt never fully set to rest.

Four centuries separate the last words of Malachi in the Old Testament from the first words of Matthew in the New Testament. "The four hundred silent years," they are called, and that phrase marks an era bordered by disappointment with God. Did God care? Was he even alive? He seemed deaf to the Jews' prayers. Still, despite everything, they waited for a Messiah—they had no other hope.

"What else can I do?" God had asked. There was something else. What could not be won through power, he would win through suffering.

God weeps with us so that we may one day laugh with him.
—*Jürgen Moltmann*

[1]Greville MacDonald, *George MacDonald and His Wife*, 172.
[2]J. R. R. Tolkien, *The Tolkien Reader*, 68–69.

Bible references: Isaiah 54; Malachi 4; Psalm 74.

Part Three

Drawing Closer:
The Son

Chapter 13

The Descent

"SUPPOSE THERE WAS A KING who loved a humble maiden," begins a story by Kierkegaard.

The king was like no other king. Every statesman trembled before his power. No one dared breathe a word against him, for he had the strength to crush all opponents. And yet this mighty king was melted by love for a humble maiden.

How could he declare his love for her? In an odd sort of way, his very kingliness tied his hands. If he brought her to the palace and crowned her head with jewels and clothed her body in royal robes, she would surely not resist—no one dared resist him. But would she love him?

She would say she loved him, of course, but would she truly? Or would she live with him in fear, nursing a private grief for the life she had left behind. Would she be happy at his side? How could he know?

If he rode to her forest cottage in his royal carriage, with an armed escort waving bright banners, that too would overwhelm her. He did not want a cringing subject. He wanted a lover, an equal. He wanted her to *forget that he was a king and she a humble maiden and to let shared love cross over the gulf between them.*

"For it is only in love that the unequal can be made equal," concluded Kierkegaard. The king, convinced he could not elevate the maiden without crushing her freedom, resolved to *descend*. He clothed himself as a beggar and approached her cottage incognito, with a worn cloak fluttering loosely about him. It was no mere disguise, but a new identity he took on. He renounced the throne to win her hand.[1]

What Kierkegaard expressed in parable form, the apostle Paul expressed in these words about Jesus the Christ:

> Who, being in very nature God,
>   did not consider equality with God
>   something to be grasped,
> but made himself nothing,
>   taking the very nature of a servant,
>   being made in human likeness.
> And being found in appearance as a man,
>   he humbled himself
>   and became obedient to death—
>   even death on a cross!

In his dealings with human beings, God had often humbled himself. I see the Old Testament as one long record of his "condescensions" ("to descend to be with"). God condescended in various ways to speak to Abraham, and to Moses, and to the nation of Israel and the prophets. But no condescension could match what came next, after the four hundred years of silence. God, like the king in Kierkegaard's parable, took on a new form: he became a man. It was the most shocking descent imaginable.

Fear Not

We hear the words every Christmas season at church pageants when children dress up in bathrobes and act out the story of Jesus' birth. "Fear not!" lisps the six-year-old angel, his bedsheet costume dragging the ground, his coat-hanger-frame wings flapping ever so slightly from the trembling of his body. He sneaks a glance at the script hidden in the folds of his sleeve. "Fear not, for I bring you good tidings of great joy." Already he has appeared to Zechariah (his older brother with a taped-on cotton beard) and to Mary (a freckled blonde from the second grade). He used the same greeting for both, "Fear not! . . ."

These were also God's first words to Abraham, and to Hagar, and to Isaac. "Fear not!" the angel said in greeting Gideon and the prophet Daniel. For supernatural beings, that phrase served almost as the equivalent of "Hello, how are you?" Little wonder. By the time the supernatural being spoke, the human being was usually lying face down in a cataleptic state. When God made contact with planet Earth, sometimes the supernatural encounter sounded like thunder, sometimes it stirred the air like a whirlwind, and sometimes it lit up the scene like a flash of phosphorous. Nearly always it caused fear. But the angel who visited Zechariah and Mary and Joseph heralded that God was about to appear in a form that would not frighten.

What could be less scary than a newborn baby with jerky limbs and eyes that do not quite focus? In Jesus, born in a barn or cave and laid in a feeding trough, God found at last a mode of approach that humanity need not fear. The king had cast off his robes.

Think of the condescension involved: the Incarnation, which sliced history into two parts (a fact even our calendars grudgingly acknowledge), had more animal than human witnesses. Think, too, of the risk. In the Incarnation, God spanned the vast chasm of fear that had distanced him from his human creation. But removing that barrier made Jesus vulnerable, terribly vulnerable.

> The child born in the night among beasts. The sweet breath and steaming dung of beasts. And nothing is ever the same again.
>
> Those who believe in God can never in a way be sure of him again. Once they have seen him in a stable, they can never be sure where he will appear or to what lengths he will go or to what ludicrous depths of self-humiliation he will descend in his wild pursuit of man. . . .

For those who believe in God, it means, this birth, that God himself is never safe from us, and maybe that is the dark side of Christmas, the terror of the silence. He comes in such a way that we can always turn him down, as we could crack the baby's skull like an eggshell or nail him up when he gets too big for that.[2]

How did Christmas day feel to God? Imagine for a moment becoming a baby again: giving up language and muscle coordination, and the ability to eat solid food and control your bladder. God as a fetus! Or imagine yourself becoming a sea slug—that analogy is probably closer. On that day in Bethlehem, the Maker of All That Is took form as a helpless, dependent newborn.

"Kenosis" is the technical word theologians use to describe Christ emptying himself of the advantages of deity. Ironically, while the emptying involved much humiliation, it also involved a kind of freedom. I have spoken of the "disadvantages" of infinity. A physical body freed Christ to act on a human scale, without those "disadvantages." He could say what he wanted without his voice blasting the treetops. He could express anger by calling King Herod a fox or by reaching for a bullwhip in the temple, rather than shaking the earth with his stormy presence. And he could talk to anyone—a prostitute, a blind man, a widow, a leper— without first having to announce, "Fear not!"

'Twas much, that man was made like God before,
But that God should be made like man, much more.
—John Donne, "Holy Sonnet 15"

[1] Paraphrase of Søren Kierkegaard, *Philosophical Fragments*, 31–43.
[2] Frederick Buechner, *The Hungering Dark*, 13–14.

Bible reference: Philippians 2.

Chapter 14

Great Expectations

EVERY YEAR around Christmastime the air vibrates with lyrical promises of the Messiah. From high school choristers to distinguished professionals, musicians trek to practices as if on a pilgrimage, clutching sheet music tattered from overuse. Nowadays you don't even have to belong to a choir to sing the famous prophecies that Handel set to music; most major cities offer a "Do-It-Yourself *Messiah*" (amazing phrase!) open to all.

And what is it that we celebrate in grand concert style? These are the words Handel lifted from the biblical prophets:

Every valley shall be exalted, and every mountain and hill made low; the crooked straight, and the rough places plain.

The people that walked in darkness have seen a great light: and they that dwell in the land of the shadow of death, upon them hath the light shined.

For unto us a Child is born, unto us a Son is given, and the government shall be upon His shoulder: and His name shall be called Wonderful, Counsellor, the Mighty God, the Everlasting Father, the Prince of Peace.

Those same words were on the lips of faithful Jews during the years of God's silence. Disappointment, even despair, metastasized throughout Israel as history, ever crueler, destroyed all hopes but one: the prophets' promise of a King of Kings. When the Messiah comes, then at last justice will roll down like a river—the Jews clung to that promise fiercely, like capsized sailors clinging to a life raft.

Four centuries after the last biblical prophet, strange rumors started circulating: first about a desert prophet named John, and then about Jesus, a carpenter's son from Nazareth. As word of Jesus' miraculous powers began to leak out, speculation spread. Could he be the One? Some insisted the Messiah truly had come. With their own eyes they had seen Jesus heal the blind and make the lame walk. "God has come to help his people!" they declared when he raised a young man from death. Others remained skeptical. Jesus fulfilled the messianic promises, but—an important but—not in the way anyone expected.

When I went through the Bible searching for signs of disappointment with God, I expected to find a decisive change when I reached the Gospels. The prophets' Messiah—as a quick scan of Handel's libretto easily shows—would seem to dispel such feelings. To the contrary, disappointment did not vanish from the earth in Jesus' day, and has not vanished yet, two thousand years later. What went wrong? Or, ask the question another way: What did Jesus' life contribute to the three questions that stalk this book?

Is God silent? "Follow me!" "This, then, is how you should pray." "We are going up to Jerusalem." In certain respects, Jesus made God's will clearer than it had ever been before. Incredibly, he opened himself to the scientific method of investigation, which is exactly what he got from Pharisees, Sadducees, and other skeptics. Anyone could walk right up to the Son of God and ask a question or debate with him. As the Gospels tell it, God broke his silence loudly and convincingly while Jesus lived on earth: the Word was made flesh.

Is God hidden? With Jesus, God actually took on a shape in the world, acquiring a face, a name, and an address. He was a God you could touch and smell and hear and see. "Anyone who has seen me has seen the Father," Jesus said bluntly.

And yet Jesus' visibility, his very ordinariness, introduced a new problem for Jews raised on stories of Mount Sinai and Mount Carmel. Where was the smoke, the fire, the burst of light? Jesus did not match their image of what God should look like. He was a man, for goodness' sake, one who hailed from the jerkwater town of Nazareth at that—Mary's boy, a common carpenter. Jesus' neighbors, who had watched him play in the streets with their own children, never could accept him as the Messiah. And Mark notes in a remarkable aside that even Jesus' own family once concluded, "He is out of his mind." His mother and brothers! Mary, who on seeing the angel Gabriel had spontaneously let loose with the annunciation hymn; his brothers, who had spent more time with him than anyone else—these, too, could not reconcile the strange combination of wondrous and ordinary. Jesus' skin got in the way.

Is God unfair? Perhaps this lingering question produced the most doubt about Jesus, for Jews believed the Messiah would set right all that was wrong with the world. Had not the prophets promised the Lord would swallow up death forever and wipe the tears from all faces? Indeed, Jesus did heal some people; but many more went unhealed. He raised Lazarus from the dead, but many others died during his time on earth. He did not wipe away tears from all faces.

The problem of unfairness bothers many people who are otherwise attracted to Jesus' life. The great theologian Augustine, for example, puzzled over the arbitrariness of the healings in the

Gospels. If Jesus had the power, why didn't he heal everyone? One story especially, from the Gospel of John, caught Augustine's attention.

The disabled of Jerusalem—the blind, the lame, the paralyzed—used to flock around a certain pool in the city, the Lourdes shrine of its day. Sometimes the water in the pool would ripple, and they would run, limp, or crawl to enter the water while it was astir. One day Jesus struck up a conversation with a pathetic man who lay there. He had been crippled for thirty-eight years, he told Jesus, but he had never made it to the pool. Whenever the waters stirred, someone would always push in ahead. Without batting an eye, Jesus ordered the invalid to get up and walk. "At once the man was cured; he picked up his mat and walked." After thirty-eight years of lying flat, he walked! He was the happiest man in Jerusalem.

But the storyteller, John, adds one significant detail: Jesus then slipped away, into the crowd. He ignored the rest of that great throng of disabled people, leaving all but the one unhealed. Why? Augustine wondered: "There lay so many there, and yet only one was healed, whilst He could by a word have raised them all up."[1]

Jesus' cousin was another person troubled by unfairness. John the Baptist, a true believer if there ever was one, had excited the nation's hopes about Jesus. In the early days, when people used to ask if John himself was the Messiah, he would set them straight: "After me will come one more powerful than I, the thongs of whose sandals I am not worthy to stoop down and untie." That promised one—Jesus of Nazareth—came to John for baptism, and he watched in amazement as the Spirit of God descended from the sky in the form of a dove. As if to eliminate all doubts about Jesus, a voice spoke from heaven, loud as thunder.

Two years later, however, John the Baptist had his own doubts, his own crisis of disappointment. Although he had served God faithfully, he had ended up in Herod's prison. While languishing on death row, he smuggled out a message to Jesus: "Are you the one who was to come, or should we expect someone else?" That single question—from John!—captures the ambivalence, the hope-yet-uncertainty, that swirled around Jesus.

The Kingdom Within

If Jesus had just avoided one emotionally charged word, *kingdom*, everything might have been different. As soon as he said it, images sprang to life in the minds of his audience: bright banners, glittering armies, the gold and ivory of Solomon's day, a nation restored to grandeur. But then something would happen to dash those expectations and all the feelings of disappointment would wash in again. As it turned out, the word *kingdom* meant one thing to the crowd and quite another to Jesus.

The masses wanted more than a sprinkling of miracles here and there; they wanted a visible kingdom of power and glory. But Jesus talked instead about "the kingdom of heaven," an invisible kingdom. Yes, he solved some problems in the world around him, but mainly he used his energy to battle unseen forces. He once encountered a paralytic so desperate for healing that the man had persuaded four friends to dig up a roof and lower him through the hole to Jesus. Jesus' response: "Which is easier, to say to the paralytic, 'Your sins are forgiven,' or to say, 'Get up, take your mat and walk'?" He made plain which was easier. No physical deformity could withstand his healing touch. The real battle was against invisible, spiritual powers.

Faith, the forgiveness of sins, the power of the Evil One—these were the concerns that drove Jesus to his Father in prayer each day. Such an emphasis confused the crowds, who primarily sought solutions to their problems in the physical world: poverty, illness, political oppression. In the end, Jesus failed to measure up to their expectations of a king. (Has anything changed? I know of many ministries that emphasize physical healing and prosperity, but few that direct their focus to such persistent human problems as pride, hypocrisy, and legalism—the problems that so troubled Jesus.)

Whatever notions Jesus' followers had of a new and mighty Solomon recapturing Israel evaporated as they watched what took

111

place in Jerusalem. A few days after a "triumphal procession"—a slapstick comedy affair compared to the lavish parades of the Romans—Jesus was arrested and put on trial. He told the Roman governor that he was in fact a king, but added, "My kingdom is not of this world. If it were, my servants would fight to prevent my arrest by the Jews. But now my kingdom is from another place."

Jesus a king? A mock king if ever there was one, with his purple robe clotted with blood from the beatings and a crown of thorns jammed onto his head. The disciples ran away, their loyalty overwhelmed by their fear of immediate danger. If Jesus would not protect himself, why should he protect them? The visible world of Roman might met the invisible world of the kingdom of heaven and seemed for a time to snuff it out.

In Cat's Cradle *the contemporary novelist Kurt Vonnegut shows a physicist who helped father the atomic bomb visiting his laboratory during the Christmas season. Office employees are all standing around a crèche singing Christmas carols. "The hopes and fears of all the years are met in thee tonight," they sing. It is a scene of biting irony, a modern counterpart to Jewish disillusionment in Jesus' day. Do the carolers really believe that the hopes and fears of all the years—which will vanish in a moment if someone presses the wrong button—rest on faith in a Bethlehem newborn destined to live only thirty-three years?*

[1] Colin Brown, Miracles and the Critical Mind, 10.

Bible references: Luke 7; John 14; Mark 3; John 5; John 1; Matthew 11; John 18.

Chapter 15

Divine Shyness

My project is the first scientific experiment in history to settle once and for all the question of God's existence. As things presently stand, there may be signs of his existence but they point both ways and are therefore ambiguous and so prove nothing. For example, the wonders of the universe do not convince those most conversant with the wonders, the scientists themselves. Whether or not this testifies to the stupidity of scientists or to God's success at concealing himself doesn't matter.

—Walker Percy, The Second Coming

IF EVER the time was ripe to settle the question of God's existence, it was while Jesus walked on earth. Jesus had one splendid opportunity to silence the critics forever.

If, for example, my friend Richard had lived in Jesus' day, he could have demanded proof to Jesus' face. "You say you're the Son of God? Okay, show me!" We need not speculate about what would have happened, for Jesus often faced a similar challenge.

When religious experts begged him for a miraculous sign, he turned on them in anger, calling them a "wicked and adulterous generation." When a curious king asked to see a miracle, Jesus refused to cooperate though it might have saved his life.

Why the divine restraint? Perhaps a clue can be found in the first "event" in Jesus' ministry, the Temptation, a kind of final exam to prepare him for public life.

You couldn't ask for a more dramatic confrontation: Jesus versus the ultimate skeptic, Satan himself, with the cracked and wrinkled hills of Palestine serving as a backdrop. Satan wanted some proof: "If you are the Son of God . . ." He challenged Jesus to make bread from a stone, asked to see a sample of Jesus' powers of self-protection, and offered him authority over all the kingdoms of the world.

I believe that Satan's challenge was a true temptation for Jesus, not a staged, predetermined contest. A loaf of bread would tempt anyone who had fasted for forty days. A guarantee of physical safety surely held appeal for someone facing torture and execution. And the splendor of all the kingdoms of earth—had not the prophets predicted as much for the Messiah? All three of the "temptations" lay within Jesus' grasp; all three were, in fact, his prerogatives. In effect, Satan was offering him a shortcut to achieve his messianic goals.

Russian novelist Fyodor Dostoyevsky made the Temptation scene a centerpiece in his masterwork *The Brothers Karamazov*. Ivan Karamazov calls the Temptation the most stupendous miracle on earth: the miracle of restraint. If he had yielded to the Temptation, Jesus would have earned his credentials, not just with Satan but with all Israel, establishing himself beyond dispute. According to Dostoyevsky's view, Satan offered three easy means of inciting belief—miracle, mystery, and authority—and Christ refused all three. In Ivan Karamazov's words, "You would not enslave man by a miracle, and craved faith given freely, not based on miracle."[1]

As I studied Matthew's concise account of the Temptation and then Dostoyevsky's long, embellished reconstruction, a question arose, abruptly, disturbingly. How does the Temptation in the desert differ from what took place in Richard's suburban apartment? He too pleaded for a supernatural display: a light, a voice, *something* that would demonstrate God's power beyond dispute. Or, getting more personal, how does the Temptation differ from times when I beg, almost demand, that God intervene and save me from a predicament?

There are differences, of course, and my self-defense quickly fills them in. Richard was, presumably, sincere; I was needy; we were both asking God for help, not taunting him or demanding worship. And yet I cannot easily dismiss the haunting similarity between Satan's "Throw yourself down!" and Richard's "Show yourself!" In each case the challenge is the same: a demand for God to take off the wraps and prove himself. In each case, God demurred.

One more instance of divine restraint comes to mind. It occurred in Jerusalem very near the site of Satan's third challenge. Jesus looked down from a high hill and cried out, "O Jerusalem, Jerusalem, you who kill the prophets and stone those sent to you, how often I have longed to gather your children together, as a hen gathers her chicks under her wings, but you were not willing!" That wail of grief over Jerusalem has about it a quality almost like shyness. Jesus, who could destroy Jerusalem with a word, who could call down legions of angels to force subjection, instead looks over the city and weeps.

God holds back; he hides himself; he weeps. Why? Because he desires what power can never win. He is a king who wants not subservience, but love. Thus, rather than mowing down Jerusalem, Rome, and every other worldly power, he chose the slow, hard way of Incarnation, love, and death. A conquest from within.

George MacDonald summed up Christ's approach: "Instead of crushing the power of evil by divine force; instead of compelling justice and destroying the wicked; instead of making peace on the earth by the rule of a perfect prince; instead of gathering the children of Jerusalem under His wings whether they would or not, and saving them from the horrors that anguished His prophetic soul—He let evil work its will while it lived; He contented

Himself with the slow unencouraging ways of help essential; making men good; casting out, not merely controlling Satan. . . . To love righteousness is to make it grow, not to avenge it. . . . Throughout His life on earth, He resisted every impulse to work more rapidly for a lower good—strong, perhaps, when He saw old age and innocence and righteousness trodden under foot."[2]

The Miracles

I have not told the whole story about Jesus, of course. Yes, his humanity represented a kind of disguise, at least in contrast to God's glory in the Old Testament. Yes, Jesus showed restraint, refusing to overwhelm people with a brash display of power. But what about the miracles he did perform, three dozen of which are recounted in the Gospels? No one who saw him provide lunch for five thousand, or order Lazarus from his tomb, or shout down a summer squall could easily speak of a quality like "divine shyness."

Yet Jesus, who presumably could work a wonder any day of his life if he wanted, seemed curiously ambivalent about miracles. With his disciples, he used them as proof of who he was ("Believe me when I say that I am in the Father and the Father is in me; or at least believe on the evidence of the miracles themselves"). But even as he performed them, he often seemed to downplay them. When he resurrected the daughter of a Jewish VIP, he gave strict orders to keep it quiet. Mark records seven separate occasions when Jesus told a person he had healed, "Tell no one!"

Jesus knew well the shallow effect of miracles in Moses' day, and in Elijah's: they attracted crowds, yes, but rarely encouraged long-term faithfulness. He was bringing a hard message of obedience and sacrifice, not a sideshow for gawkers and sensation-seekers. (Sure enough, the true skeptics of his day—much like people today—explained away his powers. If God's voice spoke from heaven, some dismissed it as thunder. Others credited his gifts to Satan. And Jesus' staunchest enemies refused to trust him even when faced with solid evidence. Once, they assembled a formal tribunal to study a reported healing. Ignoring firsthand testimony—"One thing I do know. I was blind but now I see!"—

they hurled insults at the healed man and threw him out of court. Likewise, when Lazarus showed up alive after four days in a tomb, those enemies conspired to kill him off again.)

With remarkable consistency, the Bible's accounts show that miracles—dramatic, showstopping miracles like many of us still long for—simply do not foster deep faith. For proof, we need look no further than the Transfiguration, when Jesus' face shone like the sun and his clothes became dazzling, "whiter than anyone in the world could bleach them." To the disciples' astonishment, two long-dead giants of Jewish history—Moses and Elijah—appeared in a cloud with them. God spoke audibly. It was too much to take; the disciples fell down, terrified.

Yet what effect did this stupendous event have on Jesus' three closest friends, Peter, James, and John? Did it permanently silence their questions and fill them with faith? A few weeks later, when Jesus needed them the most, they all forsook him.

3

I have read books on signs and wonders that presume to silence doubters, as if Jesus' miracles prove he is the answer to the world's problems. But I must confess that most of these arguments strike me as irrelevant to people disappointed in God. They are more interested in the miracles Jesus did *not* perform. Why does a God who possesses the power to right what is wrong sometimes choose not to? Or, why did Jesus bother with miracles at all? Why heal one paralyzed man at Bethesda—but only one?

A hint may be found in a fanciful depiction of Jesus' life that never made it into the Bible, for good reason. The spurious *Gospel of the Infancy of Jesus Christ* purports to reveal unknown stories about Jesus' childhood. It shows Jesus as a person might *want* him to be. According to this ancient book, he would perform "tricks" on demand to impress his friends—something the real Jesus always refused to do. The apocryphal Jesus had the allure of a pet genie or a neighborhood magician. Whenever his father Joseph messed up an important carpentry assignment, Jesus would step in and magically repair the flaw.

This mythical Jesus was not afraid to use his power for revenge, either. When a neighbor woman hurt one of Jesus' playmates, she mysteriously fell into a well and died of a crushed skull. When Jesus approached a town, its idols disintegrated into mounds of sand.

These hotheaded actions are uncharacteristic of Jesus as depicted in the Gospels, who used his powers compassionately to meet human needs, not for showy tricks. Every time someone asked directly, he healed. When his audience got hungry he fed them, and when wedding guests grew thirsty he made wine. The real Jesus rebuked his disciples for suggesting that he avenge a resistant city. And when soldiers came to arrest him, he used his supernatural power only once—to restore the slashed ear of one of the arresters. In short, the miracles in the authentic Gospels are about love, not power.

Although Jesus' miracles were far too selective to solve every human disappointment, they served as *signs* of his mission, previews of what God would someday do for all creation. In Helmut Thielicke's words, the miracles were "signal fires which announce the coming kingdom of God." For people who experienced them—the paralytic lowered like a chandelier for cleaning—the healings offered convincing proof that God himself was visiting earth. For everyone else, they awakened longings that will not be fulfilled until a final restoration ends all pain and death.

The miracles did just what Jesus had predicted. To those who chose to believe him, they gave even more reason to believe. But for those determined to deny him, the miracles made little difference. Some things just have to be believed to be seen.

[1]Fyodor Dostoyevsky, *The Brothers Karamazov*, 235.
[2]George MacDonald, *Life Essential: The Hope of the Gospel*, 24.

Bible references: Matthew 12, 16; Luke 4; Matthew 23 and Luke 13; John 14, 9; Mark 9.

Chapter 16

The Postponed Miracle

WHEN CHARLEMAGNE, king of the Franks, first heard the story of Jesus' arrest and execution, he exploded in rage. Grabbing his sword and rattling it in the scabbard, he shouted, "Oh, if only I had been there; I would have slain them all with my legions!" We smile at the simple warrior loyalty of Charlemagne, or of Simon Peter, who actually drew a sword in Jesus' defense. Yet behind their outrage lies a dark, dark question. Charlemagne, after all, was not present in Gethsemane and could not have helped. But God the Father, who *could* have helped, did not lift a finger on behalf of his condemned Son.

Why didn't God act? Anyone who thinks about disappointment with God must pause at Gethsemane, and at Pilate's palace, and at Calvary—the scenes of Jesus' arrest, trial, and execution. For in those three places Jesus himself experienced a state very much like disappointment with God.

The ordeal began as Jesus prayed in a quiet, cool grove of olive trees, with three of his disciples waiting sleepily outside. Inside the garden all seemed peaceful; but outside, the forces of hell itself were loose. A disciple had turned traitor, Satan was on the prowl, and a large mob with swords and clubs was heading toward Gethsemane.

"My soul is overwhelmed with sorrow to the point of death," Jesus said to his three disciples. Although he claimed the authority to dispatch an army of angels in his own defense, Jesus did not. He had come to live in a world of skin and blood and tissue, and he would die by its rules as well. At one point he fell facedown on the ground and prayed for some way, *any* way, out. His sweat fell to the ground in large drops, like blood.

And God stayed silent.

At Pilate's palace, the restraint continued. In the most literal way, God—in Jesus—had his hands tied. "Prophesy!" some cried, taunting him with a challenge toward miracle. "Who hit you?" The Son of God did not resist as their fists fell on his blindfolded face and their spit ran down his beard.

The next scene, at Calvary, has been imagined for us so many times in passion plays and sermons and paintings that, benumbed, we can hardly imagine it for ourselves. Start by remembering your time of most acute disappointment. You staked everything on what seemed within God's power—a recovery from cancer, perhaps, or the birth of a healthy baby, or God's help in stitching a marriage together. But everything turned out wrong. The cancer killed, despite your prayers; the baby was born with brain damage; you got divorce papers in the mail. Think of Calvary as that time. Or as a time like the night Richard spent in his apartment, kneeling on the floor, pleading with God. Think of it as a time of No Miracle.

Everybody craved a miracle then: Pilate and Herod, who had heard the sensational rumors; the women who had trailed Jesus all the way from Galilee; the disciples who cowered in the shadows. One dying thief begged for a miracle; the other mocked, and spectators took up the cry, "Let him come down from the cross, and we will believe in him. . . . Let God rescue him now if he wants him."

But there was no rescue, no miracle. There was only silence. Charles Williams looks back on the scene and says, "The taunt flung at Christ, at the moment of his most spectacular impotency, was: 'He saved others; himself he cannot save.' It was a definition as precise as any in the works of the medieval schoolmen."[1]

"My God, my God, why have you forsaken me?" Jesus cried out at last. It was a quotation from the Psalms, the ultimate wail of disappointment. The Father had turned his back, or so it surely seemed, letting history take its course, letting all that was wrong with the world triumph over all that was right. Nature itself convulsed: the ground shook as in an earthquake, tombs cracked open. The solar system shuddered in the chill: the sun hid, and the sky went black.

Sunday Morning

Two days later came the Resurrection, with a sound like an earthquake and a flash like lightning. Shouldn't that have vindicated God and solved the problem of disappointment once and for all?

What a missed opportunity! If only the risen Jesus had reappeared on Pilate's porch to deliver a withering blast against his enemies—that would have showed them! But his dozen or so appearances after resurrection show a clear pattern: Christ presented himself only to people who already believed in him. So far as we know, not a single unbeliever saw Jesus after his death.

Consider two men who could have seen the risen Christ, if they had tarried long enough. These coarse Roman guards were standing outside the tomb when the Miracle of Miracles occurred. They trembled and became like dead men. Then, showing an incurably human reflex, they ran to the authorities; and later that afternoon these two, the only witnesses to the actual event of resurrection, agreed to a cover-up. Stacks of freshly minted silver seemed far more significant than the resurrection of the Son of

God. And so the two eyewitnesses of that great day, the forgotten men of Easter, died apparent unbelievers.

3

Today, the major events of Jesus' life are marked on calendars around the world—Christmas, Good Friday, and Easter. Of the three, however, only the middle one, the Crucifixion, took place in the open for all the world to see. At the moment when God seemed downright helpless, the cameras of history were rolling, recording it all. Large crowds watched every excruciating detail. And when four men wrote up accounts of Jesus' life, they collectively devoted one- third of their Gospels to that time of apparent failure.

The spectacle of the Cross, the most public event of Jesus' life, reveals the vast difference between a god who proves himself through power and One who proves himself through love. Other gods, Roman gods, for example, enforced worship: in Jesus' own lifetime, some Jews were slaughtered for not bowing down to Caesar. But Jesus Christ never forced anyone to believe in him. He preferred to act by appeal, drawing people out of themselves and toward him.

Paradoxically, that scene of weakness inspired new hope. "If God is for us, who can be against us?" concluded the apostle Paul, resting his faith in the boundless love of a God "who did not spare his own Son, but gave him up for us all." Love is most persuasive when it involves sacrifice, and the Gospels make clear that Jesus came to die. In his own words, "Greater love has no one than this, that one lay down his life for his friends." Somehow, the possibility of eternal happiness required this time of silence and profound disappointment.

[1]Charles Williams, *He Came Down from Heaven*, 115.

Bible references: Matthew 26–27; Romans 8; John 15.

Chapter 17

Progress

"Madame," I said, "if our God were a pagan god or the god of intellectuals—and for me it comes to much the same—He might fly to His remotest heaven and our grief would force Him down to earth again. But you know that our God came to be among us. Shake your fist at Him, spit in His face, scourge Him, and finally crucify Him: what does it matter? My daughter, it's already been done to Him."

—George Bernanos, *Diary of a Country Priest*

L ET ME BE BLUNT: What difference does Jesus make to our feelings of disappointment with God? How does it help us to learn that he too tasted disappointment?

Theologians, following the apostle Paul, usually explain Christ's contribution in legal terms: justification, reconciliation, propitiation. But these words merely hint at what took place. To understand the difference Jesus makes to the problem of disappointment, we must look past such words to the underlying story of God's passionate pursuit of human beings.

Think back to one of the main images in the Prophets: an anxious father grieving over his runaway child. Jesus' story of the Prodigal Son provides a happy ending at last. The Waiting Father has waited long enough; he flings open the front door and *races* to welcome home the runaway, no questions asked.

The Torn Curtain

What difference did Jesus make? Both for God and for us, he made possible an *intimacy* that had never before existed. In the Old Testament, Israelites who touched the sacred Ark of the Covenant fell down dead; but people who touched Jesus, the Son of God in flesh, came away healed. To Jews who would not pronounce or even spell out the letters in God's name, Jesus taught a new way of addressing God: *Abba*, or "Daddy." In Jesus, God came close.

Augustine's *Confessions* describes how this closeness affected him. From Greek philosophy he had learned about a perfect, timeless, incorruptible God, but he could not fathom how an oversexed, undisciplined person like himself could relate to such a God. He tried various heresies of the day and found them all unsatisfying, until he met at last the Jesus of the Gospels, a bridge between ordinary human beings and a perfect God.

The Book of Hebrews explores this startling new advance in intimacy. First the author elaborates on what was required just to approach God in Old Testament times. Only once a year, on the Day of Atonement—Yom Kippur—could one person, the high priest, enter the Most Holy Place. The ceremony involved ritual baths, special clothing, and five separate animal sacrifices; and still the priest entered the Most Holy Place in fear. He wore bells on his robe and a rope around his ankle so that if he died and the bells stopped ringing, other priests could pull out his body.

Hebrews draws the vivid contrast: we can now "approach the throne of grace with confidence," without fear. Charging boldly into the Most Holy Place—no image could hold more shock value for Jewish readers. Yet at the moment of Jesus' death, a thick curtain inside the temple literally ripped in two from top to bottom, breaking open the Most Holy Place. Therefore, concludes Hebrews, "Let us draw near to God."

Jesus contributes at least this to the problem of disappointment with God: because of him, we can come to God directly. We need no human mediator, for God himself became one.

A Face

No one in the Old Testament could claim to know the face of God. No one, in fact, could survive a direct gaze. The few who caught a glimpse of God's glory came away glowing like extraterrestrials, and all who saw them hid in fear. But Jesus offered a long, slow look at the face of God. "Anyone who has seen me has seen the Father," he said. Whatever Jesus is, God is. As Michael Ramsey put it, "In God is no unChristlikeness at all."

People grow up with all sorts of notions of what God is like. They may see God as an Enemy, or a Policeman, or even an Abusive Parent. Or perhaps they do not see God at all, and only hear his silence. Because of Jesus, however, we no longer have to wonder how God feels or what he is like. When in doubt, we can look at Jesus to correct our blurry vision.

If I wonder how God views deformed or disabled people, I can watch Jesus among the crippled, the blind, and those with leprosy. If I wonder about the poor, and whether God has destined them to lives of misery, I can read Jesus' words in the Sermon on the Mount. And if I ever wonder about the appropriate "spiritual" response to pain and suffering, I can note how Jesus responded to his own: with fear and trembling, with loud cries and tears.

Not Yet

I could not help noticing an abrupt mood shift in the Bible around the Book of Acts. If you scour the rest of the New Testament, you will find none of the outrage of Job nor the despair of Ecclesiastes nor the anguish of Lamentations. Clearly, the writers of the New Testament were convinced that Jesus had changed the universe forever. The apostle Paul, for example, spraying sentence fragments across the page, spared no superlative: "In Christ all things hold together . . . through him he reconciled all things to himself, whether things on earth or things in heaven. . . . Christ is seated far above all rule and authority, power and dominion, and every title that can be given, not only in the present age but also in the one to come."

Yet as he was writing those very words, the Roman Empire was grinding on with its grim succession of wars and tyrants; people everywhere were still lying and stealing and killing each other; diseases continued to spread; and Christians themselves were being lashed with whips and thrown in jail. Such common reasons for doubt and disappointment did not seem to shake the apostles' confidence that Jesus would come again as he had promised, in power and great glory. It was simply a matter of time. They had doubted him once, but after the Resurrection they would not doubt him again.

The sure, settled tone of the New Testament writers creates a problem, though: the problem of why, some twenty centuries after the apostle Paul, I am devoting an entire book to the topic of disappointment with God. And the people who told me their wrenching stories—why do they lack the bold assurance of the New Testament writers? Why hasn't all our disappointment melted away?

As I think about these things, I keep coming back to the single question of unfairness. *Is God unfair?* In a remarkable way, Jesus gave a direct response to the problems of God's hiddenness and silence. But the problem of unfairness only seemed to worsen. Jesus' own life ended in the greatest unfairness of history: the best man who ever lived suffering the worst of punishments. One more victim of a cruel planet. Conditions hardly improved after his death, when Jesus' disciples received the "rewards" of prison, torture, and martyrdom. The problem of unfairness did not disappear.

Amazingly, the author of Hebrews seemed to anticipate that very situation, almost as a backhanded acknowledgment that people would continue to feel disappointed in God. Chapter 2 begins with a lofty quotation from the Psalms about God putting everything under Jesus' feet. Then follows this single, pregnant sentence: "Yet at present we do not see everything subject to him."

As an author, I know what it's like to write what I believe to be true and then wonder, as soon as I've written it, *Do I really mean that?* The author of Hebrews, after recording the gust of grand theology from the Psalms, likewise seems to pause and reconsider. Yes, it's true that Jesus is in control—but it sure doesn't look like it: "at present we do not see everything subject to him." That one sentence encompasses all unfairness: all war and violence, all hatred and lust, all triumph of evil over good, all illness and death, all tears and groans, all the disappointment and despair of this chaotic world. It may be the "truest" sentence in the Bible.

The paragraph continues, "But we see Jesus . . . who suffered death, so that by the grace of God he might taste death for everyone." Pointedly, Hebrews does not summon up a triumphant image of Jesus on the Mount of Transfiguration or in his resurrected body; it shows Jesus on the cross. Then the author goes on to use some of the most mysterious language of the New Testament. He tells of Christ "being made perfect" and "learning obedience" through the things that he suffered. Commentators often skirt these phrases, for they are not easy to reconcile with traditional notions of an unchanging, passionless God. But I must not skirt them, for they are presented in Hebrews as Jesus' direct contribution to the continuing problem of disappointment with God.

From Hebrews, it seems clear that the Incarnation had meaning for God as well as for us. It was the ultimate way for him to identify with us. He, a spirit, had never before been confined in the world of matter, had never experienced the soft vulnerability of human flesh, had never sensed the clamorous warnings from pain cells. Jesus changed all that. He went through the entire human experience, from the blood and pain of birth to the blood and pain of death.

From the Old Testament we can gain much insight into what it "feels like" to be God. But the New Testament records what happened when God learned what it feels like to be a human being. Whatever we feel, God felt. Instinctively, we want a God who not only knows about pain but shares in it; we want a God who is affected by our own pain. As the young theologian Dietrich Bonhoeffer scribbled on a note in a Nazi prison camp, "Only the Suffering God can help." Because of Jesus, we have such a God. Hebrews reports that God can now sympathize with our weaknesses. The very word expresses how it was done: "sympathy" comes from two Greek words, *sym pathos*, meaning "suffer with."

Would it be too much to say that, because of Jesus, God understands our feelings of disappointment with him? How else can we interpret Jesus' tears, or his cry from the cross? One could almost pour the three questions of this book into that dreadful cry, "My God, my God, why have you forsaken me?" God's Son "learned obedience" from his suffering, says Hebrews. A person can only learn obedience when tempted to disobey, can only learn courage when tempted to flee.

Why didn't Jesus brandish a sword in Gethsemane, or call on his legions of angels? Why did he decline Satan's challenge to dazzle the world? For this reason: if he had done so, he would have failed in his most important mission—to become one of us, to live and die as one of us. It was the only way God could work "within the rules" he had set up at Creation.

All through the Bible, especially in the Prophets, we see a conflict raging within God. On the one hand he passionately loved the people he had made; on the other hand, he had a terrible urge to destroy the Evil that enslaved them. On the cross, God resolved that inner conflict, for there his Son absorbed the destructive force and transformed it into love.

The only ultimate way to conquer evil is to let it be smothered within a willing, living, human being. When it is absorbed there, like blood in a sponge or a spear thrown into one's heart, it loses its power and goes no further.

— Gale D. Webbe, *The Night and Nothing*

Bible references: Hebrews 4, 10; John 14; Colossians 1; Ephesians 1; Hebrews 2–5.

Part Four

Turning It Over: The Spirit

Chapter 18

The Transfer

Y OUR STOMACH is churning with that first-day-on-the-job tension. *Will I make it? What if I do the wrong thing? Will the boss like me?* You glance around at the others who are squinting against the bright sun, shifting from one leg to the other, nervously carving designs in the sand with the edges of their sandals. Seventy of you received the summons to appear for a special assignment.

Jesus is giving a full-fledged speech. He looks worried, and his words convey alarm: "I am sending you out like lambs among wolves. Do not take a purse or bag or sandals; and do not greet anyone on the road." By the time he gets to the closing line, his voice has risen in timbre, commanding attention: "He who listens to you listens to me; he who rejects you rejects me; but he who rejects me rejects him who sent me." What is that supposed to mean? The group begins to disperse, and, swallowing your uncertainties, you head out with your designated partner on the assigned mission.

The next time you see Jesus, a few days later, it looks as if he

133

has changed faces. All severity and alarm have drained away. He's grinning at your stories, urging you to elaborate. He can't seem to get enough details about the healings and the exorcisms and the transformed lives. It really did work, this perilous mission into the hill country, and Jesus is jubilant. It's a victory party. Listen to him long enough and you'll believe you can do anything: trample on snakes, scorpions, whatever.

Right in the middle of your report he holds up his hand to interrupt. He can't wait. You've never seen him so excited. "I saw Satan fall like lightning from heaven!" he announces, and though you have no clue to what he means, you are swept up in the sudden rush of enthusiasm. Some enormous breakthrough must have just occurred. Then he bends closer and says in a hushed voice, "Many prophets and kings wanted to see what you see but did not see it, and to hear what you hear but did not hear it."

Final Exam

Another scene, about six months later. This time you are dining with the rest of the Twelve in a small room in Jerusalem. A stuffy, cloistered feeling pervades the place, and you are a bit light-headed after the meal and the wine. Everything's happening too fast. Earlier this week Jesus, permitting a rare display of public acclaim, rode into the city in a triumphant procession. It seemed all your dreams would come true after all. But tonight's mood is foreboding.

First came the incident of the foot-washing, when Jesus embarrassed Peter. And even now as he talks, Jesus' mood wavers. One minute he seems nostalgic and comforting, and the next minute he suddenly rebukes you for dullness and lack of faith. He keeps alluding to a betrayal. Some of it you do not grasp. But one thing he insists on, over all protests: he is leaving. Someone else will come to take his place; someone he calls the Counselor.

There is a sudden stirring in the room, like wind over grass. For months you have waited for Jesus to take command of his kingdom. But now he says he is turning the whole thing over—to you, the Twelve! He looks around the table and says with finality, "I confer on you a kingdom, just as my Father conferred one on me."

Departure

Okay, you failed—all of you, even Peter, who had bragged about his loyalty just a few hours before the great denial. "I have overcome the world!" Jesus had said in the small room that night. But you simply could not reconcile his words with what happened next. Less than twenty-four hours later you saw him hanging naked on a cross, his frail body glimmering in the torchlight. This one, the Savior of your nation, the King of Kings? It was too much to ask anyone to believe.

That was Friday.

On Sunday, wild, crazy rumors shot through the close-knit community of mourners. And then later in the week you saw him. It was true! You touched him with your own hands. Jesus! He had done what no one had done before: he had walked voluntarily into death, and walked back out. You would never, never doubt him again.

For forty days Jesus appeared and disappeared seemingly at will. When he showed up, you listened eagerly to his explanations of what had happened. When he left, you and the others plotted the new kingdom. Think of it: Jerusalem free at last from Roman rule!

Friends had long mocked your stubborn obsession with this peasant preacher. Now you'd show them. No one would push you around anymore; no one would push Israel around. Peter, James, and John would naturally have the inside track on the top positions, but a kingdom would need many leaders—and, after all, you had followed Jesus for three years. The Messiah, the true Messiah, had counted you among his most intimate disciples.

During those forty days, none of the glow wore off. How could it? Every reappearance of Jesus was a new miracle. At last someone broke the question to him, the burning question you had all been debating. "Lord, are you at this time going to restore the kingdom to Israel?" You waited breathless for some sign—a call to arms perhaps, a battle plan. The Romans wouldn't walk away without a fight.

No one was prepared for Jesus' reaction. At first it seemed he hadn't heard the question well. He brushed it aside and began talking not about Israel, but about neighboring countries and other faraway places. He said you were to go there eventually as his witnesses. But for now, you should simply return to Jerusalem and wait for the Holy Spirit.

Then the most amazing thing happened. You were standing there, listening to him, when suddenly his body began to lift off the ground. He hung in midair for a moment; then a cloud hid him from sight. And you never saw Jesus again.

Three Scenes

These scenes—the Sending of the Seventy, the Last Supper, and the Ascension—all reveal something about why Jesus came to earth, and why he left. True, he came to settle divine justice and to show us what God is like. But he also came to establish a Church, a new dwelling place for the Spirit of God.

And that is why, when the seventy reported back to him, Jesus nearly erupted with joy. "He who listens to you listens to me," he had told them, and indeed the plan was working. His own mission—more, his own life—was being lived out through seventy commonplace human beings.

At the last supper with the disciples, Jesus conveyed a greater sense of urgency. They were his closest friends in all the world, and it was time to turn the entire mission over to them—these well-meaning friends so quick with their protestations of loyalty now, so quick with their denials later. "As the Father has sent me, I am sending you," he said, knowing they did not comprehend. This little band would take his message to Jerusalem, and to all Judea and Samaria, and then to places he himself had never visited—all the way to the ends of the earth.

At the Ascension, Jesus' body left the earth before his astonished disciples' eyes. But soon, very soon, at Pentecost, the Spirit of God would take up residence in other bodies. Their bodies.

Bible references: Luke 10; John 13–17; Acts 1.

Chapter 19

Changes in the Wind

A documentary film series about religion for PBS. Great. One more yawner of an assignment. "Explore images of the deity through the ages," or some such abstraction, they say. Just fine. Who comes up with these schemes? For starters, the central character is invisible.

Well, until someone finds a way to arrange an interview with God himself, they'll have to settle for vignettes *about* God.

14th Century B.C. *Begin with helicopter shot of the Sinai peaks. Uninhabited area, so no TV antennae to dismantle, etc. Zoom to a clump of Bedouin extras impersonating ancient Hebrews. Voice-over on how they eat, what they wear. In tight on a Jewish boy about twelve years old. Interrupt him from play and call him over.*

"Tell me about your God. What's he like?" narrator asks.

Boy's eyes widen. "You mean . . . you mean . . ." Can't bring himself to say the word.

"That's right, Yahweh, the God you worship."

"What's he like? Him? See that mountain over there? [*Cut to volcano. Lots of steam, smoke. Close-up of magma.*] That's where he lives. Don't go near it or you'll die! He's . . . he's . . . well, most of all he's scary. *Real* scary."

A.D. *1st Century. Pan across a broad, flat horizon of Palestine. Same Bedouins, now milling around the desert in a group. Oasis in the background. Tighten in on a clump of bystanders, then on a woman along the edge, sitting down, leaning against a desert shrub. Prompt her.*

"God? I'm still trying to figure him out. I thought I knew, but when I started following this teacher around, I got confused. He claims he's the Messiah. My friends laugh. But I was in the crowd the day he fed five thousand people—who else could do that? I ate a piece of the fish. And with my own eyes I saw him heal a blind man.

"Somehow God is like that man named Jesus, over there."

A.D. *20th Century. Move film crew to picturesque church in small town, U.S.A. Pan across the faces of people in the pews.*

Voice-over from narrator, "And what is God like now?"

The New Testament asks us to believe that the answer lies in that ordinary church, among those ordinary people in the pews. God in Christ is one thing, but in *us*? The only way to sense the shock of it is to read the Bible straight through, from Genesis to Revelation, as I did during those snowy days in Colorado.

The mighty, awesome Lord of the Universe, full of passion and fire and holiness, dominates the first nine hundred pages. Four Gospels follow, about one hundred pages long, recounting Jesus' life on earth. But after Acts, the Bible shifts to a series of personal letters. Grecians, Romans, Jews, slaves, slave owners, women, men, children—the letters address all these diverse groups, and yet each letter assumes its readers belong to an overarching new identity. They are all "in Christ."

"The Church is nothing but a section of humanity in which Christ has really taken form," said Dietrich Bonhoeffer. The apostle Paul expressed much the same thought with his phrase "the body of Christ." The way he saw it, a new species of

138

humanity was emerging on earth, in whom God himself—the Holy Spirit—was living. They extended the arms and legs and eyes of God on earth. What's more, Paul acted as if that had been God's goal all along.

"Don't you know that you yourself are God's temple and that God's Spirit lives in you?" Paul wrote to the unruly bunch at Corinth. To the Jews, of course, the temple was an actual building, the central place on earth where the Presence of God dwelt. Was Paul claiming, to put it plainly, that God had "moved?"

Three temples appear in the Bible, and, taken together, they illustrate a progression: God revealed himself first as Father, then as Son, and finally as Holy Spirit.* The first temple was a magnificent structure built by Solomon and rebuilt by Herod. The second was the "temple" of Jesus' body ("Destroy it," he said, "and I will raise it again in three days"). And now a third temple has taken shape, fashioned out of individual human beings.

Delegation

> He seems to do nothing of Himself which He can possibly delegate to His creatures. He commands us to do slowly and blunderingly what He could do perfectly and in the twinkling of an eye.
>
> Creation seems to be delegation through and through. I suppose this is because He is a giver.[1]

The progression—Father, Son, Spirit—represents a profound advance in intimacy. At Sinai the people shrank from God, and begged Moses to approach him on their behalf. But in Jesus' day people could hold a conversation with the Son of God; they could

---

*I realize the Trinity is by no means a simple doctrine, and activities of the Son and the Spirit can be traced throughout the Old Testament. But we would probably not speak of a Trinity at all apart from the Incarnation and Pentecost. Each event revealed something about God that had not been known before, and each caused an upheaval in the way people thought about God.

touch him, and even hurt him. And after Pentecost the same flawed disciples who had fled from Jesus' trial became carriers of the Living God. In an act of delegation beyond fathom, Jesus turned over the kingdom of God to the likes of his disciples—and to us.

But enough. All these misty ideas about the Spirit must somehow accord with the glaring reality of the actual church. Look at the people in the pews of any church. Is this what God had in mind?

Delegation always entails risk, as any employer soon learns. When you turn over a job, you let go. And when God "makes his appeal through us" (Paul's phrase), he takes an awful risk: the risk that we will badly misrepresent him. Slavery, the Crusades, pogroms against the Jews, colonialism, wars, the Ku Klux Klan— all these movements have claimed the sanction of Christ for their cause. The world God wants to love, the world God is appealing to, may never see him; our own faces may get in the way.

Yet God took that risk, and because he did so the world will know him primarily through Christians. The doctrine of the Holy Spirit is the doctrine of "the church": God living in us. Such a plan is the "foolishness of God," as Paul says in one place, and writer Frederick Buechner marvels at the folly: "to choose for his holy work in the world . . . lamebrains and misfits and nitpickers and holier-than-thous and stuffed shirts and odd ducks and egomaniacs and milquetoasts and closet sensualists."[2]

"And yet," Paul continues, "the foolishness of God is wiser than men."

We who live among the flawed, ordinary people of the church, we who *are* the lamebrains and misfits and odd ducks of the church, may want to water down the Bible's extravagant statements about the body of Christ, for we know how poorly we embody him. But the Bible is unequivocal. Consider just two examples.

1. *We represent God's holiness on earth.* Holiness, above all else, constitutes the great distance between God and human beings. It's what made the Most Holy Place forbidden ground. But the New Testament insists that a seismic change has taken place.

A perfect God now lives inside very imperfect human beings. And because he respects our freedom, the Spirit in effect "subjects himself" to our behavior. The New Testament tells of a Spirit we can lie to, or grieve, or quench. And when we choose wrongly, we quite literally subject God to that wrong choice.

No passage illustrates this strange truth more forcefully than 1 Corinthians 6, a passage in which Paul scolds the randy members of the church at Corinth for hiring prostitutes. One by one, he smashes all their rationalizations. Then, finally, he settles on the most sobering warning of all: "Do you not know that your bodies are members of Christ himself?" Paul seems to mean this in the most literal sense, and he does not shrink from the next, astounding conclusion: "Shall I then take the members of Christ and unite them with a prostitute? Never!"

You don't have to be a biblical scholar to see the contrast. In the Old Testament, adulterers were stoned to death for disobeying God's law. But in the age of the Spirit, God delegates his reputation, even his essence, to us. We incarnate God in the world; what happens to us happens to him.

2. Human beings do the work of God on earth. Or, to be strictly accurate, God does his work through us—the tension comes into play as soon as you try to phrase it. "Without God, we cannot. Without us, God will not," said Augustine. In a similar vein, Paul wrote, "Continue to work out your salvation with fear and trembling," in one clause, and "for it is God who works in you" in the next. Whatever else they mean, such conundrums surely contradict a "Leave it up to God" attitude.

God miraculously provided food for the Israelites wandering through the Sinai desert, and even made sure their shoes would not wear out. Jesus, too, fed hungry people and ministered directly to their needs. Many Christians who read those thrilling stories look back with a sense of nostalgia, or even disappointment. "Why doesn't God act like that now?" they wonder. "Why doesn't he miraculously provide for my needs?"

But the New Testament letters seem to show a different pattern at work. Locked in a cold dungeon, Paul turned to his long-time friend Timothy to meet his physical needs. "Bring my cloak and my scrolls," he wrote, "and also bring Mark, who has always been so helpful." In other straits, Paul received "God's comfort" in the form of a visit from Titus. And when a famine broke out in Jerusalem, Paul himself led a fund-raising effort among all the churches he had founded. God was meeting the needs of the young church as surely as he had met the needs of the Israelites, but he was doing so indirectly, through fellow members of his body. Paul made no such distinction as "the church did this, but God did that." Such a division would miss the point he had made so often. The church is Christ's body; therefore if the church did it, God did it.

Paul's insistence on this truth may trace back to his first, dramatic personal encounter with God. At the time, he was a fierce persecutor of Christians, a notorious bounty hunter. But on the road to Damascus he saw a light bright enough to blind him for three days, and heard a voice from heaven: "Saul, Saul, why do you persecute me?"

Persecute you? Persecute who? I'm only after those heretics the Christians.

"Who are you, Lord?" asked Saul at last, knocked flat on the ground.

"I am Jesus, whom you are persecuting," came the reply.

That sentence summarizes as well as anything the change brought about by the Holy Spirit. Jesus had been executed months before. It was the Christians Saul was after, not Jesus. But Jesus, alive again, informed Saul that those people were in fact his own body. What hurt them, hurt him. It was a lesson the apostle Paul would never forget.

I must not leave this thought without applying its meaning in a most personal way. The doctrine of the Holy Spirit has great significance for the underlying questions of this book. My friend Richard had asked, "Where is God? Show me. I want to see him." Surely at least part of the answer to his question is this: *If you want*

142

to see God, then look at the people who belong to him—they are his "bodies." They are the body of Christ.

"His disciples will have to look more saved if I am to believe in their Savior," said Nietzsche to such a challenge. But maybe if Richard could find a saint, someone like Mother Teresa, to embody the qualities of love and grace, maybe then he would believe. *There—see her? That is what God is like. She is doing the work of God.*

Richard does not know Mother Teresa, but he does know me. And that is the most humbling aspect of the doctrine of the Holy Spirit. Richard probably will never hear a voice from a whirlwind that drowns out all questions. He will likely never get a personal glimpse of God in this life. He will only see me.

[1]C. S. Lewis, *The World's Last Night*, 9.
[2]Frederick Buechner, *A Room Called Remember*, 142.

Bible references: 1 Corinthians 3; John 2; 2 Corinthians 5; Philippians 2; 2 Timothy 4; 2 Corinthians 7; Romans 15; Acts 9.

Chapter 20

The Culmination

I F WE COULD, for a moment, set aside preconceptions about the Bible and simply read that huge book as an unfolding story, the plot line might emerge as something like this:

In the beginning God, a Spirit, created the vast world of matter. Of all God's remarkable works, only human beings possessed a likeness to him that could be called "the image of God." It was at once a great gift and a great burden, this image of God. Man and woman, spirit-ual beings, could commune directly with God. But of all species they alone had the freedom to rebel against him.

Rebel they did, and something died inside Adam and Eve that fateful day. Their bodies lived on for many years, but their spirits lost the free and open communion with God.

The Bible tells of God's efforts to restore that fallen spirit. He worked with individual families: first Adam's family, later Noah's, and finally Abraham's family, the central focus of most of the Old Testament. Sometimes the Bible portrays God as a parent raising a child, sometimes as a lover in passionate pursuit, but always it shows him seeking to "break through" to human beings in order to restore what had been lost.

With a few glowing exceptions, the Old Testament recounts failures. But the New Testament opens with a radical move by God: an "invasion," the birth of Jesus. Jesus represented a whole new beginning. "The second Adam" he was called, the leader of a new species. He at last tore down the barriers and made possible a truce between God and humanity.

After Jesus had left, at Pentecost the Spirit of God descended and filled individual human beings. Thus their fallen spirit was finally restored. More than walking in a garden with human beings, God was now living inside them.

You don't have to read far in the New Testament letters to catch the excitement. The apostle Paul could not have expressed it more strongly: "The creation waits in eager expectation for the sons of God to be revealed." He pictured the entire universe pausing to watch the events on earth: "[God's] intent was that now, *through the church*, the manifold wisdom of God should be made known to the rulers and authorities in the heavenly realms." Peter added breathlessly that "even angels long to look into these things."

Meanwhile, the little band of Christians spread out toward Samaria, Greece, Ethiopia, Rome, and Spain. According to the New Testament, they were engaged in the great reversal of history, helping to reclaim all of creation for God.

Why Better?

I determined from the outset of this book to be honest; I am writing, after all, for victims of overwrought promises and dashed expectations. So I must state frankly that it is difficult for disappointed people to share the enthusiasm of the New Testament writers. My friend Richard, for example, claims he lost his faith because God acts all too subtly. He longs for something more convincing, something along the lines of a burning bush, perhaps, or the parting of the Red Sea. The "manifold wisdom of God" being made known through the church? Have you been to a church lately? Jesus would have been impressive; the shekinah glory cloud would have stopped you flat; but the church?

How can we reconcile the exalted words of the New Testament with the everyday reality around us? Some people have a quick reply: "Oh, but Paul was talking about the New Testament church; we've strayed far from that ideal." I cannot agree. The Epistles were written to a motley crew of converted angel worshipers, thieves, idolaters, backbiters, and prostitutes—those were the people in whom God took up residence. Read Paul's descriptions of the supposed "ideal church" in a city like Corinth: a raucous, ornery bunch that rivals any church in history for their unholiness. And yet Paul's most stirring depiction of the church as Christ's body appears in a letter to them.

There is no way to pose the question elegantly, so I will simply ask it: What, exactly, does God's plan for the ages accomplish? If one could submit that plan to something like a "cost-benefit analysis" used by corporations, what would be the "gains" and "costs" of such a plan—for God and for us?

The church's obvious defects would seem to be the greatest cost to God. Just as he committed his name to the nation Israel and had it dragged through mud, he now commits his Spirit to flawed human beings. You don't have to look far—the church in Corinth, racism in South Africa, bloodshed in Northern Ireland, scandals among U.S. Christians—for proof that the church does not measure up to God's ideal. And the watching world judges God by those who carry his name. A large measure of disappointment with God stems from disillusionment with other Christians.

Dorothy Sayers has said that God underwent three great humiliations in his efforts to rescue the human race. The first was the Incarnation, when he took on the confines of a physical body. The second was the Cross, when he suffered the ignominy of public execution. The third humiliation, Sayers suggested, is the church. In an awesome act of self-denial, God entrusted his reputation to ordinary people.

Yet in some way invisible to us, those ordinary people filled with the Spirit are helping to restore the universe to its place under the reign of God. At our repentance, angels rejoice. By our prayers, mountains are moved. The gain to God can be seen in a passage already mentioned: Luke 10. "I saw Satan fall like lightning from heaven," Jesus exclaimed exuberantly when the seventy returned with success stories. He responded like a proud father who had just seen his children perform far above what he had ever thought possible.

We must not press the point so far as to think God "needs" our cooperation. Rather, he has chosen us as the preferred way to reclaim his creation here on earth. He uses human instruments just as my brain uses the instruments of fingers and hand and wrist to write this sentence. That is the metaphor Paul used most frequently to describe Christ's role in the world today: the Head of the body, directing its members to carry out his will.

To understand the gain to God, think back to the images from the Prophets: God as Parent and as Lover. Both those human relationships contain elements of what God has always been seeking from human beings. One word, *dependence*, holds the key—the key to what they have in common and the key to how they differ.

For a baby, dependence is everything; someone else must meet its every need or the child will die. Parents stay up all night, clean up vomit, teach toilet training, and perform other unpleasant chores out of love because they sense the child's dependence. But such a pattern cannot continue forever. An eagle stirs the nest to force its eaglets to fly; a mother covers her breast to wean her child.

No healthy parent wants a permanently dependent child on his hands. And so a father does not push his daughter around in a large carriage for life, but teaches her to walk, knowing that she may one day walk away. Good parents nudge their children from dependence toward freedom.

Lovers, however, reverse the pattern. A lover possesses complete freedom, yet chooses to give it away and become dependent. "Submit to one another," says the Bible, and any couple can tell you that's an apt description of the day-to-day process of getting along. In a healthy marriage, one submits to the other's wishes voluntarily, out of love. In an unhealthy marriage, submission becomes part of a power struggle, a tug-of-war between competing egos.

The difference between those two relationships shows, I believe, what God has been seeking in his long history with the human race. He desires not the clinging, helpless love of a child who has no choice, but the mature, freely given love of a lover. He has been "romancing" us all along.

God never got such mature love from the nation Israel. The record shows God nudging the young nation toward maturity: on the day Israel advanced into the Promised Land, the manna ceased. God had provided a new land; now it was up to the Israelites to grow their own food. In a typically childish response, Israel promptly started worshiping fertility gods. God wanted a lover; he got a permanently stunted child.

What about now, in the age of the Spirit? Does God now have a lover rather than a child? Amazingly, the New Testament seems to answer yes. This sampling of phrases from the New Testament expresses how God views us: "Christ loved the church . . . a radiant church, without stain or wrinkle or any other blemish, but holy and blameless"; "without fault in a crooked and depraved generation, in which you shine like stars in the universe"; "you who once were far away have been brought near"; "you are no longer foreigners and aliens, but . . . members of God's household . . . a dwelling in which God lives by his Spirit."

The Bible, in fact, presents the union of ordinary people with God's Spirit as the supreme achievement of creation. God's goal all along was to equip *us* to accomplish his will in the world. That slow, difficult process will one day result in the total restoration of the earth.

Our Gain

Such grand thoughts, however—agents of God, supreme achievement of creation—represent God's point of view, a vantage unavailable to us. What are the costs and gains of God's plan for us who live on earth? We still inhabit a world cursed with pain, tragedy, and disappointment. And what I have presented as a great advance in *closeness*—from the smoke of Sinai to the person of Jesus to the indwelling Holy Spirit—may, ironically, seem like God's *withdrawal* from direct involvement.

Some people pine for the "good old days" of the Old Testament when God used a more obvious, hands-on approach. The Old Testament tells of an actual contract signed by God guaranteeing physical safety and prosperity, under certain terms; the New Testament offers no such contract. The change from the visible presence of God in the wilderness to the invisible presence of the Holy Spirit involves a certain kind of loss as well. We lose the clear, sure proof that God exists. Nowadays, God does not hover over us in a cloud that we can gaze at for reassurance. For some, like Richard, this seems a great loss indeed.

In fact, God's reliance on the church almost guarantees that disappointment with God will be permanent and epidemic. In the old days, if the Hebrews wanted to know God's will about a military maneuver, or what kind of wood to use in the sanctuary, the high priests had ways of discerning the answer. But 1,275 denominations in the U.S. alone attest to the difficulty of the church agreeing on God's will about anything nowadays. The confused voice of the modern church is part of the cost, the disadvantage to living today rather than with the Hebrews in the desert or among the disciples who followed Jesus.

What, then, is the gain? The New Testament takes great pains to spell it out, especially in Hebrews, Romans, and Galatians. I can almost picture the apostle Paul, an excitable sort, responding to a question like "What is the gain?"

What, are you crazy?! The gain? Go back and read Leviticus, Numbers, and Deuteronomy at one sitting, and then we can talk. You call those "good old days"? Who wants to live like that? Do you want to spend every day of your life worrying about your eternal destiny? Do you want to scramble all day to make sure you keep all those rules? Do you want to go through long rituals and animal sacrifices and a fancy-dressed high priest just to approach God? Hey, I spent half my life trying to measure up to those demands, and you can have them. The difference between the Law and Spirit is the difference between death and life, between slavery and freedom, between perpetual childhood and growing up. Why would anyone want to go back to that?

To use Paul's own words, the Old Testament way was "the ministry that brought death, which was engraved in letters of stone." It was a mere "*schoolmaster* to lead us to Christ." Who wants to stay in kindergarten forever? As Paul said, "We are not like Moses, who would put a veil over his face to keep the Israelites from gazing at it while the radiance was fading away. . . . Now the Lord is the Spirit, and where the Spirit of the Lord is, there is freedom."

God's plan includes risk on both sides. For us, it means risking our independence by committing to follow an invisible God who requires of us faith and obedience. For God, it means risking that we, like the Israelites, may never grow up; it means risking that we may never love him. Evidently, he thought it a gamble worth taking.

A Trinity of Voices

Think of God's plan as a series of Voices. The first Voice, thunderingly loud, had certain advantages. When the Voice spoke from the trembling mountain at Sinai, or when fire licked up the altar on Mount Carmel, no one could deny it. Yet, amazingly, even those who heard the Voice and feared it—the Israelites at Sinai and at Carmel, for example—soon learned to ignore it. Its very volume got in the way. Few of them sought out that Voice; fewer still persevered when the Voice fell silent.

The Voice modulated with Jesus, the *Word* made flesh. For a few decades the Voice of God took on the timbre and volume and rural accent of a country Jew in Palestine. It was a normal human voice, and though it spoke with authority, it did not cause people to flee. Jesus' voice was soft enough to debate against, soft enough to kill.

After Jesus departed, the Voice took on new forms. On the

day of Pentecost, tongues—*tongues*—of fire fell on the faithful, and the church, God's body, began to take shape. That last Voice is as close as breath, as gentle as a whisper. It is the most vulnerable Voice of all, and the easiest to ignore. The Bible says the Spirit can be "quenched" or "grieved"—try quenching Moses' burning bush or the molten rocks of Sinai! Yet the Spirit is also the most intimate Voice. In our moments of weakness, when we do not know what to pray, the Spirit within intercedes for us with groans that words cannot express. Those groans are the early pangs of birth, the labor pains of the new creation.

The Spirit will not remove all disappointment with God. The very titles given to the Spirit—Intercessor, Helper, Counselor, Comforter—imply there will be problems. But the Spirit is also "a deposit, guaranteeing what is to come," Paul said, drawing on an earthy metaphor from the financial world. The Spirit reminds us that such disappointments are temporary, a prelude to an eternal life with God. God deemed it necessary to restore the spiritual link *before* re-creating heaven and earth.

In two places the New Testament compares being Spirit-filled with the state of drunkenness. Both states change the way you view life's trials, but there is a profound difference between them. Many people turn to drink to drown out the sadness of unemployment, illness, and personal tragedy. Inevitably, however, a drunk must awake from the fantasy world of inebriation and return to an unchanged reality. But the Spirit whispers of a new reality, a fantasy that is actually true, one into which we will awake for eternity.

Bible references: Romans 8; Ephesians 3; 1 Peter 1; 1 Corinthians 12; Ephesians 5; Philippians 2; Ephesians 2; 2 Corinthians 3; Galatians 3 (KJV); 2 Corinthians 3, 5.

BOOK II

SEEING
IN THE DARK

I said to my soul, be still, and let the dark
come upon you
Which shall be the darkness of God. . . .
I said to my soul, be still, and wait without hope
For hope would be hope for the wrong thing;
wait without love
For love would be love of the wrong thing;
there is yet faith
But the faith and the love and the hope are all
in the waiting.

—*T. S. Eliot, "East Coker"*

Chapter 21

Interrupted

RATHER LATE ONE NIGHT I sat in my basement office and began to outline the next part of this book, which I intended to be a review and summation. Over the years I had filled several file folders with miscellaneous notes on the subject of disappointment with God, and I started to sift through these scraps of paper, reviewing them in light of what I had learned from the Bible.

As I worked, I thought about the original meeting with Richard in my living room, when his three large questions had first emerged. These questions about God's fairness and silence and hiddenness had become my own and had launched my search through the Bible. When I began that search, I wanted a more active God, one who would on occasion roll up his sleeves and step into my life with visible power. At the least, I thought, I wanted a God who did not stay quite so hidden and silent, one who worked in slightly *less* mysterious ways. Surely that wasn't asking too much.

But the Bible contained some surprises: notably that such

times of frequent miracles usually did not foster long-term belief. Just the opposite—most of them stand out as examples of faith*less*ness. The more I studied the Bible, the less I longed for the "good old days" of daily manna and fireballs from heaven.

Most important, in the Bible I caught a glimpse of God's point of view. God's "goal," if one can speak in such terms, is not to overpower all skeptics with a flashy miracle; he could do that in an instant if he wished. Rather, he seeks to reconcile: to love, and to be loved. And the Bible shows a clear progression in God's efforts to break through to human beings without overwhelming them: from God the Father who hovered parentally over the Hebrews; to God the Son who taught the will of God "from the bottom up," rather than by fiat, from above; and finally, to the Holy Spirit who fills us with the literal presence of God. We who live now are not disadvantaged but wonderfully privileged, for God has chosen to rely primarily on *us* to carry out his will on earth.

I reviewed these thoughts with growing enthusiasm as I worked on my outline that night. Then, shuffling through another stack of papers, I found a letter from Meg Woodson.

I have known Meg for more than a decade. She is a devout Christian, a pastor's wife, and a very fine writer. Yet I cannot think of Meg without feeling a stab of grief.

The Woodsons had two children—Peggie and Joey—both born with cystic fibrosis. Peggie and Joey stayed skinny no matter how much food they ate. They coughed constantly and labored to breathe—twice a day Meg had to pound on their chests to clear out mucus. They spent several weeks each year in a local hospital, and both grew up knowing they would probably die before reaching adulthood. *

---

*Meg has written strong, moving books about both her children: *Following Joey Home*; *I'll Get to Heaven Before You Do!* and *The Time of Her Life.*

Joey, a bright, happy, all-American boy, died at the age of twelve. Peggie defied the odds by living much longer. I joined Meg in desperate prayers for Peggie. Although we knew of no recorded miraculous healings of cystic fibrosis, we prayed for healing anyway. Peggie survived several health crises in high school and went away to college. She seemed to grow stronger, not weaker, and our hopes rose that she would find healing after all.

But there was no miracle: Peggie died at the age of twenty-three. And that night in my basement office I came across the letter Meg had written to me after Peggie's death.

> I find myself wanting to tell you something of how Peggie died. I don't know why except that the need to talk about it is so compelling and, since I refuse to put my friends here through it more than once, I have run out of people to tell.
>
> The weekend before she went into the hospital for the last time, Peggie came home all excited about a quotation from William Barclay her minister had used. She was so taken with it that she had copied it down on a 3 x 5 card for me: "Endurance is not just the ability to bear a hard thing, but to turn it into glory." She said her minister must have had a hard week, because after he read it he banged the pulpit and then turned his back to them and cried.
>
> After Peggie had been in the hospital for a while and things were not going well, she looked around at all the paraphernalia of death to which she was attached. Then she said, "Hey, Ma, remember that quotation?" And she looked around again at all the tubes, stuck the tip of her tongue out of the corner of her mouth, nodded her head, and raised her eyes in excitement at the experiment to which she was committing herself.
>
> Her commitment held as long as her awareness of anything in the real world held. Once, the president of her college came to see her and asked if there was anything specific he could pray for. She was too weak to talk, but nodded to me to explain the Barclay quote and ask him to pray that her hard time would be turned into glory.

I was sitting beside her bed a few days before her death when suddenly she began screaming. I will never forget those shrill, piercing, primal screams. Nurses raced into the room from every direction and surrounded her with their love. "It's okay, Peggie," one said. "Jeannie's here."

The nurses stroked her body. Eventually with their words and their touches they soothed her (though as time went on and the screaming continued, they could not). I've rarely seen such compassion. Wendy, Peggie's special nurse-friend, tells me there isn't a nurse on the floor who does not have at least one patient she would give one of her lungs to save if she could.

So, it's against this background of human beings falling apart—nurses can only stay on that floor so long—because they could not do more to help, that God, who could have helped, looked down on a young woman devoted to Him, quite willing to die for Him to give Him glory, and decided to sit on His hands and let her death top the horror charts for cystic fibrosis deaths.

I tell you, Philip, it does not help to talk of the good that results from pain. Nor does it help to talk of God almost always letting the physical process of disease run its course. Because if He ever intervenes, then at every point of human suffering He makes a decision to intervene or not, and in Peggie's case His choice was to let C.F. rip. There are moments when my only responses are grief and an anger as violent as any I have ever known. Nor does expressing it dissipate it.

Peggie never complained against God. It was no pious restraint: I don't think it ever occurred to her to complain. And none of us who lived through her death with her complained at the time either. We were upheld. God's love was so real, one could not doubt it or rail against its ways.

If I've been telling you all this in an effort to come to some kind of resolution to the problem of Peggie's and my pain, perhaps I've been brought once again to the only thing that helps me experience God's love: His stroking, His "I'm here, Meg." But, again I wonder, how could He be in a situation like that and sit on His hands?

As I think of it, I've never expressed all this to anyone before, for fear of disturbing someone's faith. Don't think you must say anything to "make me feel better." But thanks for listening. Most people have no idea how much that helps.

After reading Meg's letter, I could not work anymore that evening.

The View from Here

Old questions churned up again, my own questions about social injustices, unanswered prayers, unhealed bodies, and countless other instances of unfairness. And Richard's questions came surging back with new emotional force, a fraction of the force Meg herself must have felt as she sat helpless by her daughter's hospital bed.

I had searched the Bible for insights into what God is up to in this world and how it must feel to be God—knowing, of course, that we can never come close to comprehending such an exalted viewpoint. Meg's letter, however, pushed me in another direction and changed my whole approach to the last part of this book.

It's fine to consider God's viewing level, but what about *our* point of view? I had been exploring what it feels like to be God; Meg's letter jarred me back to what it feels like to be human. Her questions are questions of the heart, not the head. As a mother, she watched her children die slow, horrible deaths. Yet as a Christian she believes in God the loving Father. How can she fit the two together?

That night, I realized this book was not over. Theological concepts don't amount to very much unless they can speak to someone like Meg Woodson, who gropes for God's love in a world bordered by grief. I recalled a floundering minister in a John Updike novel who said, "Something's gone wrong. I have no faith. Or, rather, I have faith, but it doesn't seem to apply." How does it apply? What do we have a right to expect from God?

Then the Lord said to Satan, "Have you considered my servant Job? There is no one on earth like him; he is blameless and upright, a man who fears God and shuns evil."

—Job 1:8

Chapter 22

The Only Problem

There is one church here, so I go to it. On Sunday mornings I quit the house and wander down the hill to the white frame church in the firs. On a big Sunday there might be twenty of us there; often I am the only person under sixty, and feel as though I'm on an archaeological tour of Soviet Russia. The members are of mixed denominations; the minister is a Congregationalist, and wears a white shirt. The man knows God. Once, in the middle of the long pastoral prayer of intercession for the whole world—for the gift of wisdom to its leaders, for hope and mercy to the grieving and pained, succor to the oppressed, and God's grace to all—in the middle of this he stopped, and burst out, "Lord, we bring you these same petitions every week." After a shocked pause, he continued reading the prayer. Because of this, I like him very much.
—Annie Dillard, Holy the Firm

SO FAR, I have avoided one book in the Bible, a book that confronts the very issues raised by the Congregationalist minister, and by Richard and Meg, and almost everyone who thinks about God. Not surprisingly, then, after reading Meg's letter I found myself turning to the Book of Job.

Possibly the oldest book in the Bible, Job reads like the most modern. Its extreme portrayal—one man confronting the abyss in a universe that makes no sense—foreshadows the predicament of modern humanity. People who reject nearly everything else in the Bible keep coming back to Job for inspiration. Its recurring theme—How can a good God allow suffering?—is "the only problem worth discussing," said contemporary British novelist Muriel Spark in her book *The Only Problem.* The problem of pain is a modern obsession, the theological kryptonite of our time, and the ancient man Job expressed it as well as it has ever been expressed.

Richard complained about the loss of a fiancée and a job and a stable home life. Meg cried out in pain over the loss of a son and a daughter. Yet by any standard Job lost far more: 7000 sheep, 3000 camels, 5000 oxen, 500 donkeys, and numerous servants. Then all Job's children—seven sons and three daughters—died in one mighty gust of wind. Finally Job's health, his last consolation, failed him, as sores broke out from the soles of his feet to the top of his head. Overnight, the greatest man in all the East was reduced to the most pitiable.

Job is the Bible's prime case study of disappointment with God, and as such it seems to anticipate whatever disappointment Richard or Meg or any of us might feel. An American rabbi wrote a popular book called *When Bad Things Happen to Good People.* The Book of Job raises the ante: it portrays the very worst things happening to the very best person.

A Misreading

If you had asked me when I began my study what the Book of Job was about, I would have been quick to respond. *Job? Everybody knows what Job is about. It's the Bible's most complete treatment of the problem of suffering. It's about terrible grief and bewildering pain.* Without doubt the bulk of the book does center on the theme of suffering. Chapters 3–37 contain no action to speak of, just the opinionated dialogues of five prickly men—Job, his three friends, and the enigmatic Elihu—concerning the problem of pain. They are all trying to account for the slings and arrows of outrageous fortune that have fallen upon poor Job, who sits forlorn in the ashes of what used to be his mansion.

I now believe I misread the book—or, more accurately, didn't take into account the entire book. Despite the fact that all but a few pages of Job deal with the problem of pain, I am coming to the conclusion that Job is not really about the problem of pain. Suffering contributes the ingredients of the story, not its central theme. Just as a cake is not about eggs, flour, milk, and shortening, but uses those ingredients in the process of creating a cake, Job is not "about" suffering; it merely uses such ingredients in its larger story, which concerns even more important questions, cosmic questions. Seen as a whole, Job is primarily about *faith* in its starkest form.

I am drawn to this conclusion mainly because of the introductory "plot" in chapters 1 and 2, which reveals that Job's personal drama on earth had its origin in a cosmic drama in heaven. I once regarded Job as a profound expression of human disappointment—something on the order of Meg Woodson's letter, only longer and more detailed, and with direct biblical sanction. As I studied the book further, however, I discovered that it does not really present the human viewpoint. God is the central character in the Bible, and nowhere does this come through more clearly than in the Book of Job. I realized that I had always read it from the perspective of chapter 3 on—in other words, from Job's perspective.

Let me explain.

It helps to think of the Book of Job as a mystery play, a "whodunit" detective story. Before the play itself begins, we in the audience get a sneak preview, as if we have showed up early for a press conference in which the director explains his work (chapters 1–2). He relates the plot and describes the main characters, then tells us in advance who did what in the play, and why. In fact, he solves every mystery in the play except one: how will the main character respond? Will Job trust God or deny him?

Later, when the curtain rises, we see only the actors on stage. Confined within the play, they have no knowledge of what the director has told us in the sneak preview. We know the answer to the "whodunit" questions, but the star detective, Job, does not. He spends all his time on stage trying to discover what we already know. He scratches himself with shards of pottery and asks, "Why me? What did I do wrong? What is God trying to tell me?"

To the audience, Job's questions should be mere intellectual exercises, for we learned the answers in the prologue, the first two chapters. What did Job do wrong? Nothing. He represents the very best of the species. Didn't God himself call Job "blameless and upright, a man who fears God and shuns evil"? Why, then, is Job suffering? Not for punishment. Far from it—he has been selected as the principal player in a great contest of the heavens.

The Wager

In retrospect, I sometimes wonder how I could have misread the Book of Job so badly. Part of the reason, I think, lies in the eloquence of chapters 3–37, which express the human dilemma with such power that we can get trapped in their force field, forgetting that the questions they raise have already been answered in chapters 1 and 2. But there is yet another reason: no one knows quite what to make of the first two chapters. Even biblical scholars tend to view the prologue with embarrassment, or discount it as the addition of a later editor. The prologue shows God and Satan involved in—and you can almost see blush marks on the commentary pages—something resembling a wager. All Job's trauma traces back to, well, a kind of bet, placed by the two cosmic powers.

The trouble starts with Satan's claim that Job is a spoiled favorite, loyal only because God has "put a hedge around him." Satan scoffs that God, unworthy of love in himself, only attracts people like Job because they're "bribed" to follow him. If times ever get tough, Satan charges, such people will quickly abandon

God. When God accepts the challenge to test Satan's theory, thus consenting to let Job's response settle the issue, the calamities begin to rain down on poor, unsuspecting Job.

I would certainly not deny the strangeness of this heavenly contest. On the other hand, I cannot sidestep the account of The Wager in Job, for it offers a rare peek through the keyhole of eternity. When people experience pain, questions spill out—the very questions that tormented Job. Why me? What's going on? Does God care? Is there a God? This one time, in the raw recounting of Job's travail, we the onlookers—not Job—are granted a view behind the curtain. What we long for, the prologue to Job provides: a glimpse into how the world is run. As nowhere else in the Bible, the Book of Job shows us God's point of view, including the supernatural activity normally hidden from us.

Job has put God on trial, accusing him of unfair acts against an innocent party. Angry, satirical, betrayed, Job wanders as close to blasphemy as he can get—just to the edge. His words have a startlingly familiar ring because they are so modern. He gives voice to our most deeply felt complaints against God. But chapters 1 and 2 prove that, regardless of what Job thinks, God is not on trial in this book. Job is on trial. The point of the book is not suffering: Where is God when it hurts? The prologue dealt with that issue. The point is faith: Where is Job when it hurts? How is he responding? To understand the Book of Job, I must begin there.

> To believe in the supernatural is not simply to believe that after living a successful, material, and fairly virtuous life here one will continue to exist in the best-possible substitute for this world, or that after living a starved and stunted life here one will be compensated with all the good things one has gone without: it is to believe that the supernatural is the greatest reality here and now.
>
> —T. S. Eliot

Bible references: Job 1–2.

> What is man that you make so much of him,
>   that you give him so much attention,
> that you examine him every morning
>   and test him every moment?
> Will you never look away from me,
>   or let me alone even for an instant?
> —Job 7:17–18

Chapter 23

A Role in the Cosmos

Some say that to the gods we are like flies that boys idly swat on a summer day. Others say that not a feather from a sparrow falls to the ground without the will of the Heavenly Father.
—Thornton Wilder, *The Bridge of San Luis Rey*

T O MY FRIEND Richard, who wrote a book about Job, that ancient man seemed a larger-than-life hero who had dared arm wrestle with God Almighty. Once, after listening to Richard expound on the valor of Job, I brought up the account of The Wager. Anger rose in his face. "All I can say," he snapped, "is that Job paid one *hell* of a price just to make God feel good!"

I, too, found it hard to avoid such sentiments at first. There is no easy way around the difficulty, for the heavenly contest played itself out in Job's life in the form of marauders, firestorms, windstorms, and boils. How can God's winning a contest, *any* contest, be worth such a price? As C. G. Jung asked in his caustic book on Job, "Is it worth the lion's while to terrify the mouse?"

As I studied Job further, however, I saw that I had been harboring the wrong image of what took place. Yes, there was an arm wrestling match, but not between Job and God. Rather, *Satan* and God were the chief combatants, although—most significantly—God had designated the man Job as his stand-in. The first and last chapters make clear that Job was unknowingly performing in a cosmic showdown before spectators in the unseen world.

Disturbing the Universe

The strange scene of The Wager reminded me of a few other places where the Bible affords a brief glimpse behind the curtain. Consider, for example, Revelation 12, which depicts an even more bizarre contest: a pregnant woman, wearing the sun for a dress and twelve stars for a crown, opposes a red dragon so enormous he can dislodge a third of the stars from the sky with one sweep of his tail. The dragon lies in wait, seeking to devour the pregnant woman's child at birth. And there's more: a flight into the desert, a serpent who tries to drown the woman, and a fierce war in heaven.

Biblical commentators propose as many interpretations of the details in Revelation 12 as there are commentaries, but almost all agree that the weird images point to the great disruption in the universe caused by Jesus' birth in Bethlehem. In a sense, Revelation 12 presents another side of Christmas, adding a new set of holographic images to the familiar scenes of manger and shepherds and the slaughter of the innocents. Which is the "true" story of Christmas: Luke's pastoral version or Revelation's account of the cosmos at war? They are the same story, of course; only the level of viewing differs. Luke gives the view from earth and Revelation shades in details from the unseen world.

The two worlds come together vividly in three of Jesus' most famous stories, the parables of the lost sheep, the lost coin, and the lost son. All three make the same point: great joy breaks out in heaven when a sinner repents. Today, anyone can watch a sinner repenting, for televised Billy Graham crusades portray the scene live and in color. The camera follows a young woman as she makes her way through the stands to an area set aside for repentance and conversion. But Jesus' stories imply that far more may be going on out there: beyond that stadium scene, in a place concealed from all camera lenses, a great party has erupted, a gigantic celebration in the unseen world.

Belief in an unseen world forms a crucial dividing line of faith today. Many people get up, eat, drive their cars, work, make phone calls, tend to their children, and go to bed without giving a single thought to the existence of an unseen world. But according to the Bible, human history is far more than the rising and falling of people and nations; it is a staging ground for the battle of the universe. Hence what seems like an "ordinary" action in the seen world may have an extraordinary effect on the unseen world: a short-term mission assignment causes Satan to fall like lightning from heaven (Luke 10); a sinner's repentance sets off celestial celebration (Luke 15); a baby's birth disturbs the entire universe (Revelation 12). Much of that effect, however, remains hidden from our view—except for the occasional glimpses granted us in places like Revelation, and in Job.

An ordinary person in the seen world, Job was called upon to endure a trial with cosmic consequences. He had no glimmer of light to guide him, no hint that the unseen world cared about him, or even existed. Yet like a laboratory test animal, he was handpicked to settle one of the most urgent issues of humanity and to determine a small piece of the history of the universe.

Is it absurd to believe that one human being, a tiny dot on a tiny planet, can make a difference in the history of the universe? It certainly seemed so to Job's friends. Listen to Elihu, the last of Job's comforters:

> If you sin, how does that affect him [God]?
>> If your sins are many, what does that do to him?
> If you are righteous, what do you give to him,
>> or what does he receive from your hand?
> Your wickedness affects only a man like yourself,
>> and your righteousness only the sons of men.

Elihu, however, was flat wrong. The opening and closing chapters of Job prove that God was greatly affected by the response of one man and that cosmic issues were at stake. (Later, in a message to the prophet Ezekiel, God would point with pride to Job—along with Daniel and Noah—as one of his three favorites.)

Job's example, drawn in sharp relief, shows how life on earth affects the universe. When I began my study, I tended to avoid the "embarrassing" scene in chapter 1, but I have since come to believe that, whether drama or history, The Wager offers a message of great hope to all of us—perhaps the most powerful and enduring lesson from Job. In the end, The Wager resolved decisively that the faith of a single human being counts for very much indeed. Job affirms that our response to testing *matters*. The history of mankind—and, in fact, my own individual history of faith–is enclosed within the great drama of the history of the universe.

God has granted us "the dignity of causation," said Pascal. We may doubt, with Elihu, whether one person can make any appreciable difference. But the Bible rustles with hints that something like The Wager is played out in other believers as well. We are God's Exhibit A, his demonstration piece to the powers in the unseen world. The apostle Paul, borrowing an image from the processional of gladiators into the Colosseum, pictured himself on public display: "We have been made a spectacle to the whole universe, to angels as well as to men." And in the same letter he commented, in an astonishing aside, "Do you not know that we will judge angels?"

We humans inhabit a mere speck of a planet in the outer suburbs of a spiral galaxy that is only one of about a million million such galaxies in the observable universe, but the New Testament insists that what happens among us here will, in fact, help determine the future of that universe. Paul is emphatic: "The whole creation is on tiptoe to see the wonderful sight of the sons of God coming into their own." Natural creation, "groaning" in travail and decay, can only be set free by the transformation of human beings.

The Great Reversal

In the Christian view, all of human history takes place somewhere between the first part of Genesis and the last part of Revelation, which paint the same scene, with the same brush strokes: Paradise, a river, the luminous glory of God, and the Tree of Life. History begins and ends at the same place, and everything in between comprises the struggle to regain what was lost.*

After the fall from Paradise, history entered a new phase. Creation God had done by himself, starting with nothing and ending up with the universe in all its splendor. The new work is Re-creation, and for this God employs the very human beings who had originally spoiled his work. Creation progressed through stages: first stars, then the sky and sea, and on through plants and animals, and finally man and woman. Re-creation reverses the sequence, starting with man and woman and culminating in the restoration of all the rest.

In many ways the act of Re-creation is "harder" than creation, for it relies on flawed human beings. Surely, it has cost God more: the death of his Son. Still, God insists on healing the world from the bottom up, rather than from the top down.

As I studied Job, it struck me that The Wager was, at its heart, a stark reenactment of God's original question in creation: Will the humans choose for or against me? From God's point of view that has been the central question of history, beginning with Adam and continuing on through Job and every man and woman who has ever lived. The Wager in the Book of Job called into question the whole human experiment.

Satan denied that human beings are truly free. We have

---

*John MacQuarrie discusses our ultimate destiny in this passage from *The Humility of God*: "If the doctrine of original sin is not to have the last word, it must be confronted with a doctrine of original righteousness. After all, in the Old Testament story righteousness is more original than sin."

freedom to descend, of course—Adam and all his descendants proved that. But freedom to ascend, to believe God for no other reason than, well . . . for no reason at all? Can a person believe even when God appears to him as an enemy? Or is faith one more product of environment and circumstance? The opening chapters of Job expose Satan as the first great behaviorist: Job was *conditioned* to love God, he implied. Take away the rewards, and watch his faith crumble. The Wager put Satan's theory to the test.

I have come to see Job's trials as a crucial test of human freedom, an important issue in modern times as well. In our century, it takes faith to believe that a human being amounts to more than a combination of DNA programming, instincts of the gene pool, cultural conditioning, and the impersonal forces of history. Yet even in this behaviorist century, we want to believe differently. We want to believe that the thousand hard and easy choices we make each day somehow count. And the Book of Job insists that they do; one person's faith can make a difference. There is a role for human beings, after all, and by fulfilling that role Job set a pattern for anyone who ever faces doubt or hardship.

Very often, disappointment with God begins in Job-like circumstances. The death of a child, a tragic accident, or a loss of job may bring on the same questions Job asked. Why me? What does God have against me? Why does he seem so distant? As readers of Job's story, we can see behind the curtain to a contest being waged in the invisible world. But in our own trials, we will not have such insight. When tragedy strikes, we will live in shadow, unaware of what is transpiring in the unseen world. The drama that Job lived through will then replicate itself in our individual lives. Once again, God will let his reputation ride on the response of unpredictable human beings.

For Job, the battleground of faith involved lost possessions, lost family members, lost health. We may face a different struggle: a career failure, a floundering marriage, sexual orientation, a body shape that turns people off, not on. At such times the outer circumstances—the illness, the bank account, the run of bad luck—will seem the real struggle. We may beg God to change those circumstances. *If only I were beautiful or handsome, then everything would work out. If only I had more money—or at least a job—then I could easily believe God.*

But the more important battle, as shown in Job, takes place inside us. Will we trust God? Job teaches that at the moment when faith is hardest and *least* likely, then faith is most needed. His struggle presents a glimpse of what the Bible elsewhere spells out in detail: the remarkable truth that our choices matter, not just to us and our own destiny but, amazingly, to God himself and the universe he rules.

In short, God has granted to ordinary men and women the dignity of participating in the Great Reversal which will restore the cosmos to its pristine state. All the reasons for disappointment with God that I have mentioned in this book, as well as all cancers, all deaths, all broken relationships, all the collected groanings of our savage planet—all these imperfections will be wiped away. We may at times question God's wisdom and lose patience with his timetable. (The disciples, after all, felt bitter disappointment when Jesus rejected their dream of a physical kingdom in favor of an invisible, spiritual kingdom.) But all the prophets' lavish promises will someday come true, and we, you and I, are the ones selected to help bring that about.

No one has expressed the pain and unfairness of this world more poignantly than Job; no one has voiced disappointment with God more passionately. We must still attend to Job's complaints and to God's fierce response. But the Book of Job begins not with the complaints—the human viewpoint—but with God's point of view. In the prologue, the scene of The Wager establishes a darkly shining truth: Job—and you and I—can join the struggle to reverse all that is wrong with the universe. We can make a difference.

The Book of Job gives no satisfying answers to the question "Why?" Instead, it substitutes another question, "To what end?" By remaining faithful to God through his trials Job, crotchety, sardonic old Job, helped abolish the very pain and unfairness of this world that he had protested so vigorously. And Meg Woodson, who stubbornly clings to God's love in the shadows, even after watching two children die . . . she too is helping to reverse those wrongs.

Why the delay? Why does God let evil and pain so flagrantly exist, even thrive, on this planet? Why does he let us do slowly and blunderingly what he could do in an eyeblink?

He holds back for our sakes. Re-creation involves us; we are, in fact, at the center of his plan. The Wager, the motive behind all human history, is to develop us, not God. Our very existence announces to the powers in the universe that restoration is under way. Every act of faith by every one of the people of God is like the tolling of a bell, and a faith like Job's reverberates throughout the universe.

Our present life feels like a real fight—as if there were something really wild in the universe which we, with all our idealities and faithfulnesses, are needed to redeem.
—William James, The Will to Believe

I had far rather walk, as I do, in daily terror of eternity, than feel that this was only a children's game in which all the contestants would get equally worthless prizes in the end.
—T. S. Eliot

Bible references: Job 35; 1 Corinthians 4, 6; Romans 8
PHILLIPS.

Yet when I hoped for good, evil came;
    when I looked for light, then came darkness.
The churning inside me never stops.
                            —Job 30:26–27

Chapter 24

Is God Unfair?

The Road Less Traveled, by M. Scott Peck, opens with a blunt three-word sentence: "Life is difficult." If reduced to a single sentence, the Book of Job would express something similar, for the loud cry, "Life is unfair!" resounds from almost every page.

Unfairness is no easier for us to swallow today than it was for Job thousands of years ago. Consider the most common curse word in the English language: "God" followed by the word "damn." People say it not only in the face of great tragedy, but also when their cars won't start, when a favored sports team loses, when it rains on their picnic. That oath renders an instinctive judgment that life *ought* to be fair and that God should somehow "do a better job" of running his world.

The world as it is versus the world as it ought to be—the constant tension between those two states bursts into the open in the Book of Job. For three long, windy rounds, Job and his friends spar in a verbal boxing match. On the ground rules, they all agree:

God should reward those who do good and punish those who do evil.

Why, then, is Job, a supposedly good man, suffering so much apparent punishment? Job's friends, confident of God's fairness, defend the world as it is. "Use your common sense," they tell Job. "God would not afflict you without a cause. You must have committed some secret sin." But Job, who knows beyond doubt he has done nothing to deserve such punishment, cannot agree. He pleads innocent.

Gradually, however, the suffering wears down Job's most cherished beliefs. How can God be on his side? Job wonders. He is, after all, squatting in a heap of ashes, the ruins of his life. He is a broken, despairing man, "betrayed" by God. "Look at me and be astonished; clap your hand over your mouth," Job cries.

A crisis of faith brews inside him. Is God unfair? Such a notion calls into question everything Job believes, but how else can he explain what has happened? He looks around for other examples of unfairness and sees that evil people sometimes do prosper—they don't get punished, as he'd like to believe—while some godly people suffer. And many other people live happy, fruitful lives without ever giving a thought to God. For Job, the facts simply do not add up. "When I think about this, I am terrified; trembling seizes my body."

The reason the Book of Job seems so modern is that for us, too, the facts do not add up. Job's strident message of life's unfairness seems peculiarly suited to our own pain-racked century. Simply plug contemporary illustrations into his arguments: "innocent" but starving children in the Third World; faithful pastors imprisoned in South Africa; Christian leaders who die in their prime; Mafia dons and spoiled entertainers who profit obscenely from flouting God's rules; the millions in Western Europe who live quiet, happy lives and never give God a thought. Far from fading away, Job's questions about this world's unfairness have only grown louder and shriller. We still expect a God of love and power to follow certain rules on earth. Why doesn't he?

Is God Unfair?

Coming to Terms with Unfairness

At some point, every human being confronts the mysteries that caused Job to tremble in terror. Is God unfair?

One option seemed obvious to Job's wife: "Curse God and die!" she advised. Why hold on to a sentimental belief in a loving God when so much in life conspires against it? And in this Job-like century, more people than ever before have come to agree with her. Some Jewish writers, such as Jerzy Kosinski and Elie Wiesel, began with a strong faith in God, but saw it vaporize in the gas furnaces of the Holocaust. Face to face with history's grossest unfairness, they concluded that God must not exist. (Still, the human instinct asserts itself. Kosinski and Wiesel cannot avoid a tone of outrage, as if they too feel betrayed. They overlook the underlying issue of where our primal sense of fairness comes from. Why ought we even *expect* the world to be fair?)

Others, equally mindful of the world's unfairness, cannot bring themselves to deny God's existence. Instead, they propose another possibility: perhaps God agrees that life is unfair, but cannot do anything about it. Rabbi Harold Kushner took this approach in his best-selling book *When Bad Things Happen to Good People.* After watching his son die of the disease progeria, Kushner concluded that "even God has a hard time keeping chaos in check," and that God is "a God of justice and not of power."

According to Rabbi Kushner, God is as frustrated, even outraged, by the unfairness on this planet as anyone else, but he lacks the power to change it. Millions of readers found comfort in Kushner's portrayal of a God who seemed compassionate, albeit weak. I wonder, however, what those people make of the last five chapters of Job, which contain God's "self-defense." No other part of the Bible conveys God's power so impressively. If God is less-than-powerful, why did he choose the worst possible situation, when his power was most called into question, to insist on his omnipotence? (Elie Wiesel said of the God described by Kushner, "If that's who God is, why doesn't he resign and let someone more competent take his place?")

A third group of people evades the problem of unfairness by

looking to the future, when an exacting justice will work itself out in the universe. Unfairness is a temporary condition, they say. The Hindu doctrine of Karma, which applies a mathematical precision to this belief, calculates it may take a soul 6,800,000 incarnations to realize perfect justice. At the end of all those incarnations, a person will have experienced exactly the amount of pain and pleasure that he or she deserves.

A fourth approach is to flatly deny the problem and insist the world is fair. Echoing Job's friends, these people insist the world does run according to fixed, regular laws: good people will prosper and evil ones will fail. I encountered this point of view at the faith-healing church in Indiana, and I hear it virtually every time I watch religious television, where some evangelist promises perfect health and financial prosperity to anyone who asks for it in true faith.

Such lavish promises have obvious appeal, but they fail to account for all the facts. The babies who contract AIDS *in utero*, for example, or the roll call of persecuted saints in *Foxe's Book of Martyrs*—how do these fit into a doctrine of life's fairness?* There is nothing I would rather have said to Meg Woodson than, "The world is fair, and therefore if you pray hard enough, your daughter will not die." But I could not say that, any more than I can now say, "God took Peggie away because of something you did wrong." Both points of view are represented in the Book of Job; both are dismissed by God in the end.

It takes an Olympian leap of faith to argue that life is completely fair. More commonly, Christians respond to life's unfairness not by denying it outright, but by watering it down.

---

*One of the "apocryphal" books circulating among early Christians told the story of a woman named Thecla, a convert of the apostle Paul. Her faith supposedly warded off all attacks: wild beasts refused to eat her, and men suddenly stopped in the act of ravishing her. When her tormentors tried to burn her at the stake, a cloud of rain and hail appeared overhead and doused the flames. The book circulated widely, but one needs only to read other books of church history, like *Foxe's Book of Martyrs*, to see why Thecla's story was ultimately dismissed as apocryphal.

They, like Job's friends, search for some hidden reason behind suffering:

"God is trying to teach you something. You should feel privileged, not bitter, about your opportunity to lean on him in faith."

"Meditate on the blessings you still enjoy—at least you are alive. Are you a fair-weather believer?"

"You are undergoing a training regimen, a chance to exercise new muscles of faith. Don't worry—God will not test you beyond your endurance."

"Don't complain so loudly! You will forfeit this opportunity to demonstrate your faithfulness to non-believers."

"Someone is always worse off than you. Give thanks despite your circumstances."

Job's friends offered a version of each of these words of wisdom, and each contains an element of truth. But the Book of Job plainly shows that such "helpful advice" does nothing to answer the questions of the person in pain. It was the wrong medicine, dispensed at the wrong time.

And finally, there is one more way to explain the world's unfairness. After hearing all the alternatives, Job was driven to the conclusion I have suggested as the one-sentence summary of the entire book: *Life is unfair!* It came to Job more as a reflex reaction than a philosophy of life, and that is how it strikes anyone who suffers. "Why me?" we ask. "What have I done?"

A Modern Job

While working on this book, I made it a point to meet regularly with people who felt betrayed by God. I wanted to keep before me the actual look, the facial expressions, of disappointment and doubt. When it came time to write about the Book of Job, I decided to interview the one person I know whose life most resembles Job's, a man I will call Douglas.

To me, Douglas seems "righteous" in the same sense as Job: not perfect, of course, but a model of faithfulness. After years of training in psychotherapy, he had declined a lucrative career in favor of starting an urban ministry. Douglas's troubles began some years ago when his wife discovered a lump in her breast. Surgeons removed that breast, but two years later the cancer had spread to her lungs. Douglas took over many household and parental duties as his wife battled the debilitating effects of chemotherapy. Sometimes she couldn't hold down any food. She lost her hair. And always she felt tired and vulnerable to fear and depression.

One night, in the midst of this crisis, as Douglas was driving down a city street with his wife and twelve-year-old daughter, a drunk driver swerved across the center line and smashed head-on into their car. Douglas's wife was badly shaken, but unhurt. His daughter suffered a broken arm and severe facial cuts from windshield glass. Douglas himself received the worst injury, a massive blow to the head.

After the accident, Douglas never knew when a headache might strike. He could not work a full day, and sometimes he would become disoriented and forgetful. Worse, the accident permanently affected his vision. One eye wandered at will, refusing to focus. He developed double vision and could hardly walk down a flight of stairs without assistance. Douglas learned to cope with all his disabilities but one: he could not read more than a page or two at a time. All his life, he had loved books. Now he was restricted to the limited selections and the sluggish pace of recorded books.

When I called Douglas to ask for an interview, he suggested meeting over breakfast; and when the scheduled time came, I braced myself for a difficult morning. By then I had interviewed a dozen people and had heard the full range of disappointment with God. If anyone had a right to be angry at God, Douglas did. Just that week, his wife had gotten a dismaying report from the hospital: there was another spot on her lung.

As our meal was being served, we caught up on the details of our lives. Douglas ate with great concentration and care. Thick glasses corrected some of his vision problems, but he had to work hard at focusing just to guide his fork to his mouth. I forced myself to look directly at him as he talked, trying to ignore the distraction of his wandering eye. At last, as we finished breakfast and motioned to the waitress for more coffee, I described my book on disappointment with God. "Could you tell me about your own disappointment?" I asked. "What have you learned that might help someone else going through a difficult time?"

Douglas was silent for what seemed like a long time. He stroked his peppery gray beard and gazed off beyond my right shoulder. I fleetingly wondered if he was having a mental "gap." Finally he said, "To tell you the truth, Philip, I didn't feel any disappointment with God."

I was startled. Douglas, searingly honest, had always rejected easy formulas like the "Turn your scars into stars!" testimonials of religious television. I waited for him to explain.

"The reason is this. I learned, first through my wife's illness and then especially through the accident, not to confuse God with life. I'm no stoic. I am as upset about what happened to me as anyone could be. I feel free to curse the unfairness of life and to vent all my grief and anger. But I believe God feels the same way about that accident—grieved and angry. I don't blame him for what happened."

Douglas continued, "I have learned to see beyond the physical reality in this world to the spiritual reality. We tend to think, 'Life should be fair because God is fair.' But God is not life. And if I confuse God with the physical reality of life—by expecting constant good health, for example—then I set myself up for a crashing disappointment.

"God's existence, even his love for me, does not depend on my good health. Frankly, I've had more time and opportunity to work on my relationship with God during my impairment than before."*

There was a deep irony in that scene. For months I had been absorbed in the failures of faith, having sought out stories of people disappointed in God. I had chosen Douglas as my modern

---

*Douglas's answer reminded me of a statement by Dr. Paul Brand. To the question "Where is God when it hurts?" Dr. Brand replied, "He is in *you*, the one hurting, not in *it*, the thing that hurts."

Job, and had expected from him a bitter blast of protest. The last thing I anticipated was a graduate-school course in faith.

"If we develop a relationship with God *apart* from our life circumstances," said Douglas, "then we may be able to hang on when the physical reality breaks down. We can learn to trust God despite all the unfairness of life. Isn't that really the main point of Job?"

Although Douglas's strict separation of "physical reality" and "spiritual reality" bothered me, I found his notion intriguing. For the next hour, we worked through the Bible together, testing out his ideas. In the Sinai wilderness, God's guarantees of *physical* success—health, prosperity, and military victory—did nothing to help the Israelites' *spiritual* performance. And most heroes of the Old Testament (Abraham, Joseph, David, Elijah, Jeremiah, Daniel) went through trials much like Job's. For each of them, at times, the physical reality surely seemed to present God as the enemy. But each managed to hold on to a trust in him despite the hardships. In doing so, their faith moved from a "contract faith"—I'll follow God if he treats me well—to a relationship that could transcend any hardship.

Suddenly, Douglas glanced at his watch and realized he was already late for another appointment. He put his coat on hurriedly and stood up to leave, and then leaned forward with one final thought. "I challenge you to go home and read again the story of Jesus. Was life 'fair' to him? For me, the cross demolished for all time the basic assumption that life will be fair."

Douglas and I had started out discussing Job and ended up discussing Jesus, and that pattern stayed with me: in the Old Testament one of God's favorites suffered terrible unfairness, and in the New Testament God's own Son suffered even more.

When I returned home, I took Douglas's advice and went through the Gospels again, wondering how Jesus would have answered the direct question, "Is life unfair?" Nowhere did I find him denying unfairness. When Jesus encountered a sick person, he never delivered a lecture about "accepting your lot in life"; he healed whoever approached him. And his scathing words about the rich and powerful of his day show clearly what he thought about social inequities. The Son of God reacted to life's unfairness much like anybody else. When he met a person in pain, he was deeply moved with compassion. When his friend Lazarus died, he wept. When Jesus himself faced suffering, he recoiled from it, asking three times if there was any other way.

God responded to the question of unfairness not with words, but with a visit, an Incarnation. And Jesus offers flesh-and-blood proof of how God feels about unfairness, for he took on the "stuff" of life, the physical reality at its unfairest. He gave, in summary, a final answer to all lurking questions about the goodness of God. (It occurred to me as I read the Gospels that if all of us in his Body would spend our lives as he did—ministering to the sick, feeding the hungry, resisting the powers of evil, comforting those who mourn, and bringing the Good News of love and forgiveness—then perhaps the question "Is God unfair?" would not be asked with such urgency today.)

The Great Unfairness

Is God unfair? The answer depends on how closely we identify God and life. Surely life on earth is unfair. Douglas was correct in saying that the Cross settled that issue forever.

Author Henri Nouwen tells the story of a family he knew in Paraguay. The father, a doctor, spoke out against the military regime there and its human rights abuses. Local police took their revenge on him by arresting his teenage son and torturing him to death. Enraged townsfolk wanted to turn the boy's funeral into a huge protest march, but the doctor chose another means of protest. At the funeral, the father displayed his son's body as he had found it in the jail—naked, scarred from the electric shocks and cigarette burns and beatings. All the villagers filed past the corpse, which lay not in a coffin but on the blood-soaked mattress from the prison. It was the strongest protest imaginable, for it put injustice on grotesque display.

Isn't that what God did at Calvary? "It's God who ought to suffer, not you and me," say those who bear a grudge against God for the unfairness of life. The curse word expresses it well: God be damned. And on that day, God was damned. The cross that held Jesus' body, naked and marked with scars, exposed all the violence and injustice of this world. At once, the Cross revealed what kind of world we have and what kind of God we have: a world of gross unfairness, a God of sacrificial love.

No one is exempt from tragedy or disappointment—God himself was not exempt. Jesus offered no immunity, no way *out* of the unfairness, but rather a way *through* it to the other side. Just as Good Friday demolished the instinctive belief that this life is supposed to be fair, Easter Sunday followed with its startling clue to the riddle of the universe. Out of the darkness, a bright light shone.

The primal desire for fairness dies hard, and it should. Who among us does not sometimes yearn for more justice in this world here and now? Secretly, I admit, I yearn for a world "fault-proof" against disappointment, a world where my magazine articles will always find acceptance and my body does not grow old and weak, a world where my sister-in-law does not deliver a brain-damaged child, and where Peggie Woodson lives into ripe old age. But if I stake my faith on such a fault-proof earth, my faith will let me down. Even the greatest of miracles do not resolve the problems of this earth: all people who find physical healing eventually die.

We need more than miracle. We need a new heaven and a new earth, and until we have those, unfairness will not disappear.

A friend of mine, struggling to believe in a loving God amid much pain and sorrow, blurted out this statement: "God's only excuse is Easter!" The language is non-theological and harsh, but within that phrase lies a haunting truth. The Cross of Christ may have overcome evil, but it did not overcome unfairness. For that, Easter is required. Someday, God will restore all physical reality to its proper place under his reign. Until then, it is a good thing to remember that we live out our days on Easter Saturday.

Is God Unfair?

To be commanded to love God at all, let alone in the wilderness, is like being commanded to be well when we are sick, to sing for joy when we are dying of thirst, to run when our legs are broken. But this is the first and great commandment nonetheless. Even in the wilderness—especially in the wilderness—you shall love him.

—Frederick Buechner

Bible references: Job 21, 2.

Surely I spoke of things I did not understand,
things too wonderful for me to know.

—Job 42:3

Chapter 25

Why God Doesn't Explain

TOWARD THE END of the Book of Job, brash young Elihu delivers a stinging address in which he ridicules Job's desire for a visit from God. "Do you think God cares about a puny creature like you? Do you imagine that Almighty God, the Maker of the Universe, will deign to visit earth and meet with you in person? Does he owe you some kind of explanation? Get serious, Job!"

As Elihu drones on, a tiny cloud appears on the horizon, just over his shoulder. And as the cloud draws closer, roiling into a full-fledged storm, a Voice like no other voice booms out. Elihu's fine speech abruptly ends, and Job begins to tremble. God himself has arrived on the scene. He has come to reply in person to Job's accusations of unfairness.

If Job serves as the Bible's main case study of disappointment with God, then surely this dramatic speech out of the whirlwind should yield important insights into all other times of confusion and doubt. What, then, does God say in his own defense?

I can think of several helpful things God could have said:

189

"Job, I'm truly sorry about what's happened. You've endured many unfair trials on my behalf, and I'm proud of you. You don't know what this means to me and even to the universe." A few compliments, a dose of compassion, or at the least a brief explanation of what transpired "behind the curtain" in the unseen world—any of these would have given Job some solace.

God says nothing of the kind. His "reply," in fact, consists of more questions than answers. Sidestepping thirty-five chapters' worth of debates on the problem of pain, he plunges instead into a magnificent verbal tour of the natural world. He seems to guide Job through a private gallery of his favorite works, lingering with pride over dioramas of mountain goats, wild donkeys, ostriches, and eagles, speaking as if astonished by his own creations. The beauty of the poetry at the end of Job rivals anything in world literature. Even as I marvel at God's dazzling portrayal of the natural world, however, a sense of bewilderment steals in. Of all moments, why did God choose this one to give Job a course in wilderness appreciation? Are these words relevant?

In his book *Wishful Thinking*, Frederick Buechner sums up God's speech. "God doesn't explain. He explodes. He asks Job who he thinks he is anyway. He says that to try to explain the kind of things Job wants explained would be like trying to explain Einstein to a little-neck clam. . . . God doesn't reveal his grand design. He reveals himself."[1] The message behind the splendid poetry boils down to this: *Until you know a little more about running the physical universe, Job, don't tell me how to run the moral universe.*

"Why are you treating me so unfairly, God?" Job has whined throughout the book. "Put yourself in my place."

"NO!!!" God thunders in reply. "You put yourself in *my* place! Until you can offer lessons on how to make the sun come up each day, or where to scatter lightning bolts, or how to design a hippopotamus, don't judge how I run the world. Just shut up and listen."

The impact of God's speech on Job is almost as amazing as the speech itself. Although God never answers question one about Job's predicament, the blast from the storm flattens Job. He repents in dust and ashes, and every trace of disappointment with God is swept away.

What We Cannot Know

The rest of us, however, who may never hear a voice speaking out of the whirlwind, must try to figure out what God actually said to Job. Quite frankly, for me God's evasive reply creates as many problems as it solves. I cannot simply wish the "Why?" questions away. They come up every time I talk to someone like Meg Woodson, every time my own life starts to unravel.

God's refusal to answer Job's questions does not sit well with modern minds. We don't like—*I* don't like—being told something is beyond our grasp. I own a book titled *The Encyclopedia of Ignorance* which outlines many areas of science we cannot yet explain; but scientists all over the world are doing their best to explore those areas and fill in the gaps of knowledge. Has God perhaps fenced off an area of knowledge, *The Encyclopedia of Theological Ignorance,* that no human being will ever understand?

Much as I resist, I am pushed toward such a conclusion by the Book of Job. Why is life so unfair? When does God cause suffering and when merely permit it—and what is the difference? Why does God sometimes seem silent and sometimes close and intimate? When God had the perfect opportunity to settle those issues for good, he scowled and shook his head. Why bother to explain? Not Job nor any other human being could possibly understand.

I cannot offer answers to Job's specific questions, because God offered none. I can only ask why God gives no answers, why there must be an *Encyclopedia of Theological Ignorance.* Because I am entering an area on which the Bible stays silent, what follows is pure speculation. I include it for people who are never satisfied with a non-answer, for those who cannot stop asking questions even God has declined to answer.

1. Perhaps God keeps us ignorant because enlightenment might not help us.

The same urgent questions torment almost every suffering person: Why? Why me? What is God trying to tell me? In the

Book of Job, God deflects those questions of *cause*, and focuses instead on our *response* of faith. But think what might happen if God did answer our questions forthrightly. We assume that we would bear suffering better if we only knew the reason behind it. But would we?

I find striking similarities in two biblical books: Job and Lamentations. Job stared in disbelief at the ruins of his house and possessions; the author of Lamentations stared in disbelief at the ruins of his city, Jerusalem. Both books express anger and bitterness and deep disappointment with God. In fact, many passages from Lamentations sound like paraphrases of the much older Book of Job. Yet the prophet who wrote Lamentations (probably Jeremiah) was not in the dark. He knew exactly why Jerusalem had been destroyed: the Hebrews had broken their covenant with God. Nevertheless, knowing the cause did nothing to alleviate the suffering or the feelings of despair and abandonment. "The Lord is like an enemy," he pronounced, Job-like. "Why do you always forget us? Why do you forsake us so long?" he asked of God, though he knew full well the answers—other parts of the book spell them out in exhaustive detail.

What possible explanation could comfort a Job, a Jeremiah, or a Meg Woodson? Knowledge is passive, intellectual; suffering is active, personal. No intellectual answer will solve suffering. Perhaps this is why God sent his own Son as one response to human pain, to experience it and absorb it into himself. The Incarnation did not "solve" human suffering, but at least it was an active and personal response. In the truest sense, no words can speak more loudly than the Word.

If you look to the Book of Job for an answer to the "Why?" questions, you will come away disappointed. God declined to answer, Job withdrew his questions, and the three friends repented of all their mistaken assumptions. Jesus likewise avoided the issue of the direct cause of suffering. When his disciples drew certain conclusions about a man born blind (John 9) and about two local catastrophes (Luke 13), Jesus rebuked them. From the biblical evidence, I must conclude that any hard-and-fast answers to the "Why?" questions are, quite simply, out of reach.

Whenever we take on one of God's prerogatives, we tread on dangerous ground. Even a well-meaning attempt to comfort a child, "God took your Dad home because he liked him so much," crosses over into an area that the Bible seems to rule out of bounds. Though catastrophes—an airplane crash, a plague, a sniper's random killings, the deliberate poisoning of medicines, a famine in Africa—cry out for some authoritative interpretation, the Book of Job offers an important reminder: God himself did not attempt an explanation.

2. *Perhaps God keeps us ignorant because we are incapable of comprehending the answer.*

Maybe God's majestic non-answer to Job was no ploy, no clever way of dodging questions; maybe it was God's recognition of a plain fact of life. A tiny creature on a tiny planet in a remote galaxy simply could not fathom the grand design of the universe. You might as well try to describe colors to a person born blind, or a Mozart symphony to a person born deaf, or expound the theory of relativity to a person who doesn't even know about atoms.

To appreciate the problem, imagine yourself trying to communicate with a creature on a microscope slide. The "universe" to such a creature consists of only two dimensions, the flat plane of the glass slide; its senses cannot perceive anything beyond the edges. How could you convey a concept of space or height or depth to such a creature? Looking "from above," you can understand the creature's two-dimensional world as well as the three-dimensional world surrounding it. The creature, however, "from below," can only comprehend a world of two dimensions. *
In a similar way, the unseen world exists outside our range of perception—except for rare interventions into our "plane," which

---

*Anthropologists report a very similar "perception gap" among remote cultures. If a rural Indian in Papua New Guinea is shown a photograph of a forest, he sees only marks and splotches of colors on a flat paper. He must, through experience, learn to "see" that the two-dimensional photograph actually contains three-dimensional images: birds, trees, waterfalls.

we call miracles. Job, or you and I, cannot comprehend the total picture with our present faculties.

Filmmaker Woody Allen playfully explored this "two worlds" level of viewing in his movie *Purple Rose of Cairo*. We first see the hero through Mia Farrow's eyes as she watches him play a role in a movie. Then, incredibly, that hero steps out—literally—from the two-dimensional movie screen and lands in the New Jersey theater; suddenly he is in the "real" world with the flabbergasted character played by Miss Farrow.

The outside world holds many surprises for the movie actor. When someone hits him with a fist, he dutifully falls down, as he was taught to do on-screen, but rubs his jaw with amazement—those blows aren't supposed to hurt! When he and Mia kiss, he pauses, waiting for the fadeout. And when someone tries to explain the concept of God—"He's the one in control of everything. He's what the whole world is about"—the actor nods, "Oh, you mean Mr. Mayer, the owner of the movie company." His perceptions are confined to the world of the movie.

Eventually, the actor climbs back onto the two-dimensional movie screen and tries to explain the real world to the rest of the cast. They stare at him as if he belongs in a mental asylum. He's talking nonsense. There is no "other" world out there; only the world of the movie is real for them.

Woody Allen makes the same point as the analogy of the two-dimensional creature. If one world (the world of two-dimensions, or the world of the movie) exists inside another, it will only make sense from the "higher" world's point of view. And, to carry the analogy a long way, all the way back to the Book of Job, most of Job's questions concerned activity in the "higher" world, a world beyond his comprehension.

God lives on a "higher" level, in another dimension. The universe does not contain him; he created the universe. In a way we cannot fathom, he is not bound by space and time. He can step into the material world—if he did not, in fact, our senses would never perceive him—but it is for him a "stepping into," like an author who introduces himself as a character in his own play, like a person in the real world who makes a brief appearance in a movie.

A Matter of Time

There was a young lady named Bright
Whose speed was much greater than light
    So she set off one day
    In a relative way
And returned on the previous night.

The perception of time, especially, points up the huge difference between God's perspective (the view from above) and ours, and I have come to believe that this difference accounts for many of our unanswered questions on disappointment with God. For that reason, it merits what may seem like a diversion.

St. Augustine devoted Book 11 of *The Confessions* to a discussion of time. "What, then, is time?" he begins. "If no one asks me, I know; if I want to explain it to someone who does ask me, I do not know." When asked, "What was God doing *before* creation?" Augustine responded that since God invented time along with the created world, such a question is nonsense, and merely betrays the time-bound perspective of the questioner.* "Before" time there is only eternity, and eternity for God is a never-ending present. For God, one day is like a thousand years, and a thousand years are like a day.[2]

What would Augustine make of all that has happened since Einstein connected time and space? Now we understand time as relative, not as absolute. Perception of time, we are told, depends on the relative position of the observer. Take a recent example: on the night of February 23, 1987, an astronomer in Chile observed with his naked eye the explosion of a distant supernova, a blast so powerful that it released as much energy in one second

---

*Martin Luther was not nearly so polite. "When one asked, where God was before heaven was created? St. Augustine answered: He was in himself. When another asked me the same question, I said: He was building hell for such idle, presumptuous, fluttering and inquisitive spirits as you."

as our sun will release in ten billion years. But did that event truly occur on February 23, 1987? Only from the perspective of our planet. Actually, the supernova exploded 170,000 years prior to our 1987, but the light generated by that faraway event, traveling almost 6 trillion miles a year, took 170,000 years to reach our galaxy.

And here is where the "higher" view of eternity defies our normal understanding of time. Imagine, if you will, a very large Being, larger than the entire universe—so large that the Being exists simultaneously on earth and in the space occupied by Supernova 1987A. In 1987, *what time was it* for that Being? It depends on the perspective. From the perspective of earth, the Being would have "observed" 1987 history, which included the discovery of Supernova 1987A. But from the perspective of Supernova 1987A, the Being would have experienced what the earth will not know about for another 170,000 years! The Being thus observed both past (from earth, he saw the supernova explosion of 170,000 years before), present (the events of 1987 on earth), and future (what was happening on Supernova 1987A "now" that earthlings will not learn about for 170,000 years) simultaneously.

Such a Being, big as the universe, could, from some lookout post, see what is happening anywhere in the universe at any given time. For example, if he wants to know what is taking place on our sun right now, he can "watch" from the perspective of the sun. If he wants to see what took place on the sun eight minutes ago, he can "watch" from earth—that's what we see, after light has traveled the 93 million miles from the sun to earth.

The analogy is inexact, for it traps such a Being in space even as it frees him from time. But it may illustrate how our "first A happens, then B happens" conception of time expresses the very limited perspective of our planet. God, outside both time and space, can view what happens on earth in a way we can only guess at, and never fully comprehend.

Such notions are not mere flights of fancy. High school physics students learn about theoretical astronauts of the future who will travel into space faster than the speed of light and thus return even younger than when they left. Theories that seemed wildly speculative just a decade ago are being proved by modern researchers who bounce laser beams off the moon and send atomic clocks into space. Science is fulfilling fantasy: "It is a poor memory indeed that only works backwards!" said the White Queen to Alice in Wonderland.

God and Time

One more analogy: as a writer, I live in two different "time zones." First, there is the time zone of the real world that encompasses my daily ritual of waking, getting dressed, eating breakfast, and then moving to my office to plan out chapters, pages, and words. Meanwhile, the book itself is creating another, artificial world with its own self-contained time zone.

If I were writing a book of fiction, I might write these two sentences: "The phone rang. Immediately she got up from the couch and ran to answer it." Within the book, the time sequence goes like this: phone rings, immediate response. But outside the book, in the author's world, minutes, hours, even days may separate those two sentences. Perhaps I end one day's work with the sentence "The phone rang," and then go on vacation for two weeks. Regardless of when I return to the book, I am bound by the laws of its time zone. I could never write, "The phone rang. Two weeks later she got up and answered it." Mixing the two time zones would create an absurdity.

After I finish the book, in a way peculiar to me as its author, I carry around the entire book inside my mind. "From above," I can see the whole plot at once: beginning, middle, and end. No one else can do that—not unless they too experience it within time by plodding through it sentence by sentence.

I keep reaching for analogies because analogies are the only means we have to imagine human history as God sees it. We see history like a sequence of still frames, one after the other, as in a motion picture reel; but God sees the entire movie at once, in a flash. He sees it simultaneously from the viewpoint of a faraway star and from the viewpoint of my living room where I sit praying.

He sees it in entirety, like a whole book, rather than sentence by sentence and page by page.

We can imagine such a perspective dimly, as if through a fog. But merely recognizing our incurable time-boundedness may help us understand why God did not answer Job's "Why?" Instead, God replied by reeling off a few fundamental facts of the universe that Job could barely comprehend, and warning, "Leave the rest to me." Perhaps God keeps us ignorant because neither Job, nor Einstein, nor you or I could possibly understand the view "from above."

We cannot understand what "rules" apply to a God who lives outside of time, as we perceive it, and yet sometimes steps into time. Consider all the confusion that surrounds the word "foreknowledge." Did God know in advance whether Job would stay faithful to him and thus win The Wager? If he did, how was it a real wager? Or what about natural disasters on earth? If God knows about them in advance, isn't he to blame? In our world, if a person knows in advance that a bomb will explode in a parked car and fails to warn authorities, he or she is legally responsible. Is God therefore "responsible" for everything that happens, even tragedies, because he knows about them in advance?

But—and this may be the main message underlying God's vigorous speech to Job—we cannot apply our simplistic rules to God. The very word *fore*knowledge betrays the problem, for it expresses the B-follows-A viewpoint of someone trapped inside time. Strictly speaking, God does not "foresee" us doing things. He simply *sees* us doing them, in an eternal present. And whenever we try to figure out God's role in any given event, we necessarily see things "from below," judging his behavior by the frail standards of a time-contingent morality. One day we may see such problems as "Did God cause that airplane to crash?" in a very different light.

The church's long arguments over *fore*knowledge and *pre*destination illustrate our awkward attempts to comprehend what, to us, only makes sense as it enters time. In another dimension, we will undoubtedly view such matters very different-ly. The Bible hints at the viewpoint "from above" in some of its most mysterious passages. It says that Christ "was chosen before the creation of the world," which means before Adam and before the Fall and thus before the need for redemption at all. It says grace and eternal life were "given us in Christ Jesus before the beginning of time." How could anything be said to occur "*before* the beginning of time"? Such wording suggests the viewpoint of a God who lives outside time. Before creating time, he made provision to redeem a fallen planet that did not yet even exist! But when he "stepped into" time (as I, an author, might write myself into my own book), God had to live, and die, by the rules of our world, trapped within time.*

The Eternal Present

There is a sense in which we humans also perceive time in something like a never-ending present. True, we experience it in sequence—morning happens, then afternoon, then evening—but we do all our thinking in the present. If I think about the breakfast I ate earlier this morning, I think *in the present* about what happened in the past. If I contemplate dinner this evening, I

---

*This difference in perception may also help clarify one of the most confusing aspects of the Prophets. Often they did not bother telling whether the predicted events—invasions, earthquakes, a coming Leader, a re-created earth—would occur the next day, or a thousand years later, or three thousand years later. In fact, near and distant predictions often appear in the same paragraph, blurring together. Isaiah's famous prophecy, "Therefore the Lord himself will give you a sign: The virgin will be with child and will give birth to a son, and will call him Immanuel," fits this category. The next two verses make clear that the sign had a fulfillment in Isaiah's own day (many scholars assume the child to be Isaiah's own), and yet Matthew applies the prophecy's final fulfillment to the Virgin Mary. Biblical scholars have names for this common characteristic of the prophets: double or triple fulfillment, part-for-the-whole, creative bisociation.

For a God who encompasses all time, sequence is the least important issue. Should we be surprised, then, that incursions into time by a timeless Being would have overtones that resound in Isaiah's day, and Mary's, and also our own?

think *in the present* about what will happen in the future. Because I only exist in the present, I can only perceive the past and the future from the perspective of the present.

That insight gives a slight glimpse into the eternal present from which God "sees" the world. And it may explain the Bible's consistent pattern for people who doubt God. To such people, trapped in the present, disappointed with God, the Bible offers two cures: remember the past and consider the future. In the Psalms, in the Prophets, in the Gospels and Epistles, the Bible constantly urges us to look back and remember the great things God has done. He is the God of Abraham, Isaac, and Jacob, the One who delivered the Hebrews from slavery in Egypt. He is the God who, out of love, sent his Son to die, and who then resurrected him from death. By focusing too myopically on what we want God to do on our behalf, we may miss the significance of what he has already done.

Likewise, the Bible points us toward the future. For disappointed people everywhere—the Jews held captive in Babylon, the Christians persecuted by Rome, or by Iran or South Africa or Albania—the prophets envision a future state of peace and justice and happiness; and they call us to live in light of the future they image up. Can we live now "as if" God is loving, gracious, merciful, and all-powerful, even while the blinders of time are obscuring our vision? The prophets proclaim that history will be determined not by the past or present, but by the future.

I have taken such a long diversion into the mysteries of time because I believe there is no other answer to the question of unfairness. No matter how we rationalize, God will sometimes *seem* unfair from the perspective of a person trapped in time. Only at the end of time, after we have attained God's level of viewing, after every evil has been punished or forgiven, every illness healed, and the entire universe restored—only then will fairness reign. Then we will understand what role is played by evil, and by the Fall, and by natural law, in an "unfair" event like the death of a child. Until then, we will not know, and can only trust in a God who does know.

We remain ignorant of many details, not because God enjoys

keeping us in the dark, but because we have not the faculties to absorb so much light. At a single glance God knows what the world is about and how history will end. But we time-bound creatures have only the most primitive manner of understanding: we can let time pass. Not until history has run its course will we understand how "all things work together for good." Faith means believing in advance what will only make sense in reverse.

I have a friend who bristles at such a definition of faith: "You never blame God for the bad things and yet you give him credit for the good things!" In a curious sort of way, my friend is right. That, I believe, is also what faith sometimes requires: trusting God when there is no apparent evidence of him—as Job did. Trusting in his ultimate goodness, a goodness that exists outside of time, a goodness that time has not yet caught up with.

> *The Eternal may meet us in what is, by our present measurements, a day, or (more likely) a minute or a second; but we have touched what is not in any way commensurable with lengths of time, whether long or short. Hence our hope finally to emerge, if not altogether from time (that might not suit our humanity) at any rate from the tyranny, the unilinear poverty, of time, to ride it, not to be ridden by it, and so to cure that always aching wound which mere succession and mutability inflict on us, almost equally when we are happy and when we are unhappy. For we are so little reconciled to time that we are even astonished at it. "How he's grown!" we exclaim, "How time flies!" as though the universal form of our experience were again and again a novelty. It is as strange as if a fish were repeatedly surprised at the wetness of water. And that would be strange indeed; unless of course the fish were destined to become, one day, a land animal.*
> —C. S. Lewis, *Reflections on the Psalms*

[1]Frederick Buechner, *Wishful Thinking*, 46.
[2]Saint Augustine, *The Confessions of Saint Augustine*, 286-287.

Bible references: Job 36–38; Lamentations 2, 5; 1 Peter 1; 2 Timothy 1; Isaiah 7:14; Romans 8.

Why is life given to a man
    whose way is hidden,
    whom God has hedged in?
For sighing comes to me instead of food;
    my groans pour out like water.
                    —Job 3:23–24

Chapter 26

Is God Silent?

ONCE A FRIEND OF MINE went swimming in a large lake at dusk. As he was paddling at a leisurely pace about a hundred yards offshore, a freak evening fog rolled in across the water. Suddenly he could see nothing: no horizon, no landmarks, no objects or lights on shore. Because the fog diffused all light, he could not even make out the direction of the setting sun.

For thirty minutes he splashed around in panic. He would start off in one direction, lose confidence, and turn ninety degrees to the right. Or left—it made no difference which way he turned. He could feel his heart racing uncontrollably. He would stop and float, trying to conserve energy, and force himself to breathe slower. Then he would blindly strike out again. At last he heard a faint voice calling from shore. He pointed his body toward the sounds and followed them to safety.

Something like that sensation of utter lostness must have settled in on Job as he sat in the rubble and tried to comprehend what had happened. He too had lost all landmarks, all points of orientation. Where should he turn? God, the One who could guide him through the fog, stayed silent.

The whole point of The Wager was to keep Job in the dark. If God had delivered an inspiring pep talk—"Do this for me, Job, as a Knight of Faith, as a martyr"—then Job, ennobled, would have suffered gladly. But Satan had challenged whether Job's faith could survive with no outside help or explanation. When God accepted those terms, the fog rolled in around Job.

God ultimately "won" The Wager, of course. Though Job lashed out with a stream of bitter complaints, and though he despaired of life and longed for death, still he defiantly refused to give up on God: "Though he slay me, yet will I hope in him." Job believed when there was no reason to believe. He believed in the midst of the fog.

You could read Job's story, puzzle over The Wager, then breathe a deep sigh of relief: *Phew! God settled that problem. After proving his point so decisively, surely he will return to his preferred style of communicating clearly with his followers.* You could think so—unless, that is, you read the rest of the Bible. I hesitate to say this, because it is a hard truth and one I do not want to acknowledge, but Job stands as merely the most extreme example of what appears to be a universal law of faith. The kind of faith God values seems to develop best when everything fuzzes over, when God stays silent, when the fog rolls in.

Survivors of the Fog

A flash of light from a beacon on shore and then a long, dreadful time of silence and darkness—that is the pattern I find not only in the Book of Job, but throughout the Bible. Recall tottery old Abraham as he neared the century mark, holding feebly to the lustrous vision that he would father a great nation. For twenty-five years that vision had seemed a desert mirage until one son, just one, was born. And when God spoke again, he called Abraham to a test of faith every bit as severe as Job's. "Take your son, your only son, Isaac, whom you love," said God, in words that stabbed deep into Abraham's heart, "and sacrifice him as a burnt offering."

Then there was Joseph, who heard from God in his dreams but landed at the bottom of a well and later in an Egyptian dungeon for trying to follow that guidance. And Moses, hand-picked liberator of the Hebrew people, who hid in a desert for forty years, hunted by a pharaoh's security guards. And the fugitive David, anointed king on God's command, who spent the next decade dodging spears and sleeping in caves.

The baffling, Morse-code pattern of divine guidance—a clear message followed by a long, silent gap—is spelled out bluntly in 2 Chronicles. There we read of a rare good king, Hezekiah, who so pleased God that he was granted an unprecedented fifteen-year extension to his life. What happened next? "God *left him* to test him and to know everything that was in his heart."

Most of these Old Testament characters show up in the honor roll of Hebrews 11, a chapter some have labeled "The Faith Hall of Fame." I prefer to call that chapter, "Survivors of the Fog," for many of the heroes listed have one common experience: a dread time of testing like Job's, a time when the fog descends and everything goes blank. Torture, jeers, floggings, chains, stonings, sawings in two—Hebrews records in grim detail the trials that may befall faith-full people.

Saints become saints by somehow hanging on to the stubborn conviction that things are not as they appear, and that the unseen world is as solid and trustworthy as the visible world around them. God deserves trust, even when it looks like the world is caving in. "The world was not worthy of them," Hebrews 11 concludes about its amazing assemblage, adding this intriguing comment: "Therefore God is not ashamed to be called their God." For me, that phrase puts a reverse spin on Dorothy Sayers's remark about the three great humiliations of God—the church, in particular, has borne God shame, but it has also brought him moments of pride, and the gaunt saints of Hebrews 11 demonstrate how.

God's favorites, *especially* God's favorites, are not immune from the bewildering times when God seems silent. As Paul Tournier said, "Where there is no longer any opportunity for doubt, there is no longer any opportunity for faith either." Faith demands uncertainty, confusion. The Bible includes many proofs of God's concern—some quite spectacular—but no guarantees. A guarantee would, after all, preclude faith.

Two Kinds of Faith

My friend Richard found the word "faith" a central obstacle to belief: "Just have faith," other Christians would counsel when he doubted. What did they mean? "Faith" seemed to him a method of avoiding questions, not of answering them.

Some of the difficulty comes, I think, from the elastic way in which we use the word. First, we use it to describe great, childlike gulps of faith, when a person swallows the impossible. David exercised this kind of extravagant faith when he strode out to meet Goliath, as did the Roman centurion whom Jesus commended (he was "astonished" by the man's unflinching confidence). In our day, "faith missionaries" write stirring accounts of miracles that may result from childlike trust. This is the "seed faith" that can feed a houseful of orphans or move a mountain, and the Bible contains many proddings toward such.

But Job, along with the saints in Hebrews 11, points to a different kind of faith, the kind I have circled around in this book on disappointment with God. Childlike trust may not survive when the miracle does not come, when the urgent prayer gets no answer, when a dense gray mist obscures any sign of God's concern. Such times call for something more, and I will use the musty word "fidelity" for that hang-on-at-any-cost faith.

I interviewed a young nurse whose disappointment with God stemmed directly from confusing these two kinds of faith. Reared in a Christian home, she seldom doubted God, even through her college years. On her wall hung a painting of Jesus with a child in his arms, illustrating the poem "Footprints." That plaque portrayed faith at its most childlike: simply trust God and you will not even feel the burden. As you look back on hard times, you'll see only one set of footprints in the sand, for Jesus has carried you through.

At the age of twenty-four, this nurse was assigned to work in a cancer ward. She told me, one by one, the case histories of people she had nursed there. Some of her patients had prayed with childlike faith, crying out to God for healing and comfort, for relief from pain. Yet they died cruel, ugly deaths. And each night this nurse would come home, weighed down by the scenes of unsolvable suffering, and face the footprints plaque with its bright, alluring promise.

To get the picture vividly, simply read two psalms back-to-back. Start with Psalm 23: "The Lord is my Shepherd, I shall not be in want . . . he guides me . . . I will fear no evil . . . goodness and love will follow me all the days of my life." Then turn back one page to Psalm 22. "My God, my God, why have you forsaken me? Why are you so far from saving me? . . . I cry out by day, but you do not answer . . . I can count all my bones; people stare and gloat over me."

Psalm 23 models childlike faith; Psalm 22 models fidelity, a deeper, more mysterious kind of faith. Life with God may include both. We may experience times of unusual closeness, when every prayer is answered in an obvious way and God seems intimate and caring. And we may also experience "fog times," when God stays silent, when nothing works according to formula and all the Bible's promises seem glaringly false. Fidelity involves learning to trust that, out beyond the perimeter of fog, God still reigns and has not abandoned us, no matter how it may appear.

Paradoxically, the most perplexing, Job-like times may help "fertilize" faith and nurture intimacy with God.* The deepest faith, what I have called fidelity, sprouts at a point of contradiction, like a blade of grass between stones. Human beings grow by striving, working, stretching; and in a sense, human nature needs problems more than solutions. Why are not all prayers answered magically and instantly? Why must every convert travel the same tedious path of spiritual discipline? Because persistent prayer, and

---

*American Christians who have visited churches in places like Ethiopia and China can attest to this fact.

fasting, and study, and meditation are designed primarily for our sakes, not for God's.

Kierkegaard said that Christians reminded him of schoolboys who want to look up the answers to their math problems in the back of the book rather than work them through. I confess to such schoolboy sentiments, and I doubt that I am alone. We yearn for shortcuts. But shortcuts usually lead away from growth, not toward it. Apply the principle directly to Job: what was the final result of the testing he went through? As Rabbi Abraham Heschel observed, "Faith like Job's cannot be shaken because it is the result of having been shaken."

In an essay on prayer, C. S. Lewis suggested that God treats new Christians with a special kind of tenderness, much as a parent dotes on a newborn.[1] He quotes an experienced Christian: "I have seen many striking answers to prayer and more than one that I thought miraculous. But they usually come at the beginning before conversion, or soon after it. As the Christian life proceeds, they tend to be rarer. The refusals, too, are not only more frequent; they become more unmistakable, more emphatic."[1]

At first glance, such a suggestion seems to have it all backward. Shouldn't faith become easier, not harder, as a Christian progresses? But, as Lewis points out, the New Testament gives two strong examples of unanswered prayers: Jesus pled three times for God to "Take this cup from me" and Paul begged God to cure the "thorn in my flesh."

Lewis asks, "Does God then forsake just those who serve Him best? Well, He who served Him best of all said, near His tortured death, 'Why hast thou forsaken me?' When God becomes man, that Man, of all others, is least comforted by God, at His greatest need. There is a mystery here which, even if I had the power, I might not have the courage to explore. Meanwhile, little people like you and me, if our prayers are sometimes granted, beyond all hope and probability, had better not draw hasty conclusions to our own advantage. If we were stronger, we might be less tenderly treated. If we were braver, we might be sent, with far less help, to defend far more desperate posts in the great battle."

208

Is God Silent?

The Unavoidable Question

C. S. Lewis's words sound impressive. Yet I cannot simply reduce the pattern of fidelity—faith toughened through testing—to a cheery formula. This book began with the story of Richard, who was secure and well-grounded until his faith was tested. And then he felt betrayed. Why would God submit him or, for that matter, *anyone* he loves, to such a test? Richard could no longer trust such a God. I have spoken with many others whose exuberant, childlike faith likewise foundered in the time of testing.

An unavoidable question lurks just under the surface of the Book of Job. If, for the sake of a "test" of love, a husband subjected his wife to the trauma that Job had to endure, we would call him pathological and lock him away. If a mother hid herself from her children, refusing to call out directions from the shore in the fog, we would judge her an unfit mother. How, then, can we understand such behavior, such a wager, by God himself?

I offer no neat formula, only two observations.

1. *We have little comprehension of what our faith means to God.* In some mysterious way, Job's terrible ordeal was "worth" it to God because it went to the core of the entire human experiment. More than Job's faith, the motive behind all creation was at stake. Ever since God took the "risk" of making room for free human beings, faith—true, unbribed, freely offered faith—has had an intrinsic value to God that we can barely imagine. There is no better way for us to express love to God than by exercising fidelity to him.

It is wrong to speak of God's need of love from his creation, but remember how God himself expressed his longing for that love: like a father starved for some response, *any* response, from his rebellious children; like a jilted lover who, against all reason, gives his faithless beloved one more chance. Those are the images God summoned up again and again throughout the time of the prophets. The deepest longings we feel on earth, as parents, as lovers, are mere flickers of the hungering desire God feels for us. It is a desire that cost him the Incarnation and the Crucifixion.

All human metaphors fail to contain these matters, but they fail from understatement, not exaggeration. As Jesus said, at the end of history (when the fog lifts for good) only one question will matter: "When the Son of Man comes, will he find faith on the earth?" And the apostle Paul, after sketching out the scheme of the world from creation up to Jesus, concluded, "God did this so that men would seek him and perhaps reach out for him and find him, though he is not far from each one of us." Sending his Son was the "cost" to God; a faithful response from someone like Job—or you or me—represents the "reward."

I admit, it is hard for any of us with our limited vision to perceive the "reward" gained by Job's trials. C. S. Lewis may have come close in his comment about God sending us to "far more desperate posts in the great battle." According to the Bible, human beings serve as the principal foot soldiers in the warfare between unseen forces of good and evil; and faith is our most powerful weapon. Perhaps God sends us to dangerous posts with the same mixture of pride, love, anguish, and remorse that any parent feels when sending a son or daughter off to war.

Was Job's trial "worth it" to God? Only God can answer that. I have had to conclude that divine sovereignty means at least this: only God can determine what is of value to God. "Blessed are those who have not seen and yet have believed," Jesus said in a mild rebuke to doubting Thomas. Job saw the darkest side of life, heard the deepest silence of God, and still believed.

2. *God did not exempt himself from the same demands of faith.* Job's trials cannot stand apart from their louder echo in the life of Jesus. He too was tempted. He too lost everything of value, including his friends and his health. As Hebrews says, he "offered up prayers and petitions with loud cries and tears to the one who could save him from death." Finally, he lost his life.

We can never fully plumb the mystery of what took place on the cross, but it does offer the consolation that God is unwilling to put his creatures through any test that he himself has not endured. I have spoken with many suffering people over the years, and I cannot emphasize too strongly how important this fact seems to them. From famous people like Joni Eareckson Tada, from unknowns in county hospitals, from inmates in hellish Third World prisons, I have heard something like this: "At least, because of Jesus, God understands how I feel."

I think again of Richard's comment, "All I can say is that Job paid one *hell* of a price just to make God feel good!" He was thinking of Job, sitting in the ashes, scratching his sores. But as Richard said those words I was thinking of Jesus, hanging on a cross, unable to reach his wounds. I had to agree—it was a hell of a price to pay. In one sense, God tied his own hands in the wager over Job; in the most literal sense, he let his hands be tied the night of the Crucifixion. (Jesus, speaking of his death: "Now my heart is troubled, and what shall I say? 'Father, save me from this hour'? No, it was for this very reason I came to this hour. Father, glorify your name!")

In my study of the Bible, I was struck by a radical shift in its authors' attitudes about suffering, a shift that traces directly back to the Cross. When New Testament writers speak of hard times, they express none of the indignation that characterized Job, the prophets, and many of the psalmists. They offer no real explanation for suffering, but keep pointing to two events—the death and resurrection of Jesus—as if they form some kind of pictographic answer.

The apostles' faith, as they freely confessed, rested entirely on what happened on Easter Sunday, when God transformed the greatest tragedy in all history, the execution of his Son, into a day we now celebrate as Good Friday. Those disciples, who gazed at the cross from the shadows, soon learned what they had failed to learn in three years with their leader: When God seems absent, he may be closest of all. When God seems dead, he may be coming back to life.

The three-day pattern—tragedy, darkness, triumph—became for New Testament writers a template that can be applied to all our times of testing. We can look back on Jesus, the proof of God's love, even though we may never get an answer to our "Why?" questions. Good Friday demonstrates that God has not abandoned us to our pain. The evils and sufferings that afflict our lives are so real and so significant to God that he willed to share them and endure them himself. He too is "acquainted with grief." On that day, Jesus himself experienced the silence of God—it was Psalm 22, not Psalm 23, that he quoted from the cross.

And Easter Sunday shows that, in the end, suffering will not triumph. Therefore, "Consider it pure joy . . . whenever you face trials of many kinds," writes James; and "In this you greatly rejoice, though now for a little while you may have had to suffer grief in all kinds of trials," writes Peter; and "we also rejoice in our sufferings," writes Paul. The apostles go on to explain what good can result from such "redeemed suffering": maturity, wisdom, genuine faith, perseverance, character, and many rewards to come.

Why rejoice? Not for the masochistic thrill of the trial itself, but because what God did Easter Sunday on large scale he can do on small scale for each of us. The afflictions addressed by James, Peter, and Paul would likely have ignited a major crisis of faith in the Old Testament. But New Testament writers came to believe that, as Paul expressed it, "All things work together for good."

That well-known passage is often distorted. Some people interpret its meaning as "Only good things will happen to those who love God." Paul meant just the opposite, and in the very next paragraph he defines what "things" we might expect: trouble, hardship, persecution, famine, nakedness, danger, sword. Paul endured all those. Yet, he insists, "in all these things we are more than conquerors"; no amount of hardship can separate us from the love of God.

It's a matter of time, Paul says. Just wait: God's miracle of transforming a dark, silent Friday into Easter Sunday will someday be enlarged to cosmic scale.

Is God Silent?

Though thou with clouds of anger do disguise
Thy face; yet through that mask I know those eyes,
Which, though they turn away sometimes,
They never will despise.
　　　　　—John Donne, "A Hymn to Christ"

Everything difficult indicates something more than our theory
of life yet embraces.
　　　　　　　　　　　　　—George MacDonald

[1]C. S. Lewis, *The World's Last Night*, 10.

Bible references: Job 13; Genesis 22; 2 Chronicles 32; Matthew 8; Mark 14; 2 Corinthians 12; Luke 18; Acts 17; John 20; Hebrews 5; John 12; Isaiah 53 (KJV); James 1; 1 Peter 1; Philippians 3; Romans 8.

But if I go to the east, he is not there;
    if I go to the west, I do not find him.
When he is at work in the north, I do not see him;
    when he turns to the south, I catch no
      glimpse of him.

                     —Job 23:8–9

Chapter 27

Why God Doesn't Intervene

I KNOW WHAT my friend Richard would think about the ideas in the last few chapters. In fact, I know what he does think, because I discussed them with him at length. Richard, you may remember, had written a book on Job, so I had no need to review the story with him. I concentrated instead on the ending, speculating aloud on why God declined to answer Job. I went over my thoughts about timelessness, and Job's inability to comprehend God's perspective, and the inherent value of faith to God.

Richard listened carefully, and when I had finished meandering through my ideas, he nodded approvingly. "That's good, Philip. You may well be right. I have no problem with what you say. But there's one big difference between Job's story and mine. For all his troubles, Job finally did receive a word from God. Supposedly, he heard an actual voice out of the whirlwind. But for me, God stayed silent. And I guess that's why Job chose to believe, and I chose not to."

As we talked further, it became clear that Richard simply could not accept the notion of two worlds. Living in a seen world

215

of trees and buildings and cars and people, he could not believe in another, unseen world existing alongside it. "I want proof," he said. "How can I be certain that God even exists if he won't enter into my world?"

The conversation took me back to a time when I too was a skeptic. Richard, ironically, lost his faith at a Christian college, surrounded by believers who professed an intimate knowledge of God; and it was in a similar environment—a Bible college no less—that I found faith most difficult.

A Skeptic's View

I ran into the same stumbling block as Richard: actions regarded as "spiritual" by the believers on campus seemed utterly ordinary to me. If the unseen world really was making contact with the seen world, where were the scorch marks, the sure signs of a supernatural Presence?

Take the matter of prayer: the believers seemed to distort events to make everything look like an answer to prayer. If an uncle sent an extra fifty dollars to help with school bills, they would grin and shout and call a prayer meeting to thank God. They accepted these "answers to prayer" as final proof that God was out there listening to them. But I could always find another explanation. Perhaps the uncle had sent all his nephews fifty dollars that month, and the prayers were merely coincidental. After all, I had an uncle who occasionally sent me gifts, though I never prayed for them. And what of these students' many requests that went unanswered? Prayer, it seemed to me, involved nothing more than talking to the walls and an occasional self-fulfilling prophecy.

As an experiment, I began mimicking "spiritual" behavior on campus. I prayed devoutly in prayer meetings, gave phony testimonies about my conversion, and filled my vocabulary with pious jargon. And it worked, confirming my doubts. I the skeptic soon passed for a veritable saint, just by following the prescribed formula. Could Christian experience be genuine if most of it was reproducible by a skeptic?

216

I conducted this experiment as a result of my reading in the psychology of religion. Books like *The Varieties of Religious Experience,* by William James, had persuaded me that religion was just a complex psychological reaction to the stresses of life. James examined the claims that the sincere Christian is a new creature formed out of new fabric. But, concluded James, "Converted men as a class are indistinguishable from natural men; some natural men even excel some converted men in their fruits; and no one ignorant of doctrinal theology could guess by mere every-day inspection of the 'accidents' of the two groups of persons before him that their substance differed as much as divine differs from human substance."[1] I too could see no unusual radiance, no distinguishing mark in the believers around me.

For reasons I will explain later, I did not remain a skeptic. But in honesty I must admit that even now, after two decades of rich and rewarding faith, I am vulnerable to Richard's kind of doubt. Spiritual experience does not bear introspection easily; shine a spotlight on it, and it vaporizes. If I probe my times of communion with God, I can usually uncover another, more natural explanation for what has taken place. There is no blinding difference between the natural and supernatural worlds, no gulf fixed with barbed wire separating the two.

I do not stop being a "natural" person when I pray: I get sleepy, lose concentration, and suffer the same frustrations and miscommunications while conversing with God that I do with other people. When I write on "spiritual" topics, I am not suddenly lifted heavenward by the muses; I still must sharpen pencils, cross out words, consult the dictionary, wad up and throw away countless false starts. Instances of "knowing God's will" in my life have never been as straightforward as the examples I see in the life of a Moses or Gideon. I have never heard the booming Voice from the whirlwind. I could, if I wished, do what Richard does now: explain away spiritual behavior through some combination of psychological theories.

Why, then, do I believe in an unseen world? I have received great help in this struggle from the writings of C. S. Lewis. The theme of two worlds runs like a thread through most of his work—

in the early writings, in letters to his friends, and in all his fiction, until it finally develops into a full-blown theory in an essay called "Transposition."[2] Lewis defined the problem as being "that of the obvious continuity between things which are admittedly natural and things which, it is claimed, are spiritual; the reappearance in what professes to be our supernatural life of all the same old elements which make up our natural life." Most of what follows in this chapter will simply expand on his ideas.

Looking Along the Beam

Lewis began his essay by referring to the curious phenomenon of *glossolalia* or speaking in tongues. How odd, he commented, that an undeniably "spiritual" event, the descent of the Holy Spirit at Pentecost, would express itself in the strange human phenomenon of speaking in another language. To the bystanders at Pentecost it resembled drunkenness; to many "scientific" observers today glossolalia resembles hysteria or a nervous disorder. How can such natural actions as the movement of vocal cords express the supernatural indwelling of the Holy Spirit of God?

Lewis suggested the analogy of a beam of light in a dark toolshed. When he first entered a shed, he saw a beam and looked *at* the luminous band of brightness filled with floating specks of dust. But when he moved over to the beam and looked *along* it, he gained a very different perspective. Suddenly he saw not the beam, but, framed in the window of the shed, green leaves moving on the branches of a tree outside and beyond that, 93 million miles away, the sun. Looking at the beam and looking along the beam are quite different.

Our century excels in techniques of looking *at* the beam, and "reductionism" is the word most commonly used to describe this process. We can "reduce" human behavior down to neurotransmitters and enzymes, reduce butterflies to molecules of DNA, and reduce sunsets to particle waves of light and energy. In its most extreme forms, reductionism sees religion as psychological projection, world history as evolutionary struggle, and thought itself as

218

only the opening and shutting of billions of I/O computer gates in the brain.

This modern world, so skilled in looking at the beam from every angle, is a world hostile to "faith." Throughout most of history, all societies took for granted the existence of an unseen, supernatural world. How else could they explain such marvels as a sunrise, an eclipse, a thunderstorm? But now we can explain them, and much more. We can reduce most natural phenomena, and even most spiritual phenomena, to their component parts. As Lewis observed about glossolalia, even the most "supernatural" acts express themselves on this earth in "natural" ways.

From the theory of transposition, I draw these conclusions about living in such a world.

1. First, *we must simply acknowledge the powerful force of reductionism.* That force offers both a blessing and a curse. It blesses us with the ability to analyze earthquakes and thunderstorms and tornadoes and thus defend ourselves against them. By looking *at* the beam, we have learned to fly—all the way to the moon and back—and to tour the world while staring at a box in our living rooms, and to bring the sounds of orchestras to our ears as we jog along country lanes. By looking at the beam of human behavior, we can recognize chemical components and thus, through drugs, rescue people from severe depression and schizophrenia.

But reductionism has also brought a curse. Looking at the beam rather than along it, we risk reducing life to nothing more than its constituent parts. We will never again view the sunrise or moonrise with the same sense of awe and near-worship that our "primitive" ancestors—or even the sixteenth-century poets—felt. And if we reduce behavior to *merely* hormones and chemistry, we lose all human mystery and free will and romance. The ideals of romantic love that have inspired artists and lovers through the centuries suddenly reduce to a matter of hormonal secretions.

Reductionism may exert undue influence over us unless we recognize it for what it is: a way of looking. It is not a True or False concept; it is a point of view that informs us about the parts of a thing, but not the whole.

Spiritual acts, for example, can be viewed from both a lower and higher level. One does not supplant the other; each merely sees the same behavior differently (just as looking *at* a beam of light differs from looking *along* it). From the "lower" perspective, prayer is a person talking to himself (and glossolalia the same, only gibberish). The "higher" perspective presumes that a spiritual reality is at work, with human prayer serving as a contact point between the seen and unseen worlds.

I can attend a Billy Graham rally as a curious spectator and, selecting one person in the vast audience, theorize on all the sociological and psychological factors that might entice this one woman to be receptive to Graham's message. Her marriage is falling apart; she's looking for stability; she remembers the strength of a pious grandmother; the music takes her back to childhood church experiences. But those "natural" factors do not rule out the supernatural; to the contrary, they may be the means God chooses to prompt that person toward him. Perhaps the continuity between natural and supernatural is a continuity of design from the same Creator. That, at least, is the "higher" view of faith. The one level of viewing does not exclude the other; they are two ways of looking at the same event.

2. *Oddly, the lower viewpoint may even seem superior to the higher.* C. S. Lewis recalled that as a child he had first learned to appreciate orchestral music by listening to the single, undifferentiated sound produced by a primitive gramophone. He could hear the melody, but not much else. Later, when he went to live concerts, he was disillusioned. A multitude of sounds came from many instruments playing different notes! He longed for "the real thing," which to his untrained ear was the mongrel sound of the gramophone. To Lewis, at that moment, the substitute seemed superior to the reality.[3]

Similarly, a person raised on a steady diet of television might find real mountain hiking, complete with mosquitoes, shortness of breath, and annoying weather changes, inferior to the vicarious experience afforded by a *National Geographic* special.

More to the point, the lower viewpoint may seem superior in moral issues as well. The ideal of romantic love has inspired our greatest sonnets and novels and operas. But reductionists like Hugh Hefner now argue quite articulately that sex is superior when freed from the constraints of love and relationship. (Certainly, *Playboy* has more visceral appeal than the works of Elizabeth Barrett Browning.) And secularists, dismissing religion as a crutch, extol the "braver" challenge of surviving in this world without an appeal to a higher Being.

3. *The reality of the higher world is carried by the faculties of the lower world.* The word "transposition" belongs to the vocabulary of music. A song can be transposed from one musical key into another. Or a symphony score written for 110 orchestral instruments can be transposed into a version for the piano. Naturally, something will get lost in the process: ten fingers striking piano keys cannot possibly reproduce all the aural nuances of an orchestra. Yet the transposer, limited to the range of sounds made by those keys, must somehow convey the essence of the symphony through them.

C. S. Lewis cited a diary entry from Samuel Pepys regarding a rapturous musical concert. Pepys said the sound of the wind instruments was so sweet that it ravished him "and, indeed, in a word, did wrap up my soul so that it made me really sick, just as I have formerly been when in love with my wife." Try to analyze the physiology of any emotional response, said Lewis. What happens in our bodies when we experience beauty, or pride, or love? To Pepys it felt at once ravishing, yet not unlike nausea. A kick in the stomach, a flutter, a muscular contraction—he experienced the very same bodily reactions that he might at a moment of illness![4]

Looked at from the lower viewing level, our physical responses to joy and fear are almost identical. In each case the adrenal gland secretes the same hormone, and neurons in the digestive system fire off the same chemicals; but the brain interprets one message as joy and one as fear. At its lower levels, the human body has a limited vocabulary, just as a transposer has a limited number of piano keys to express the sounds of a full orchestra.

And this is where reductionism reveals its greatest weakness:

if you look only "at the beam," reducing human emotions to their most basic components (neurons and hormones), you might logically deduce that joy and fear are the same, when they are in fact near-opposites. The human body has no nerve cells specially assigned to convey a sensation of pleasure—nature is never so lavish. All our experiences of pleasure come from "borrowed" nerve cells that also carry sensations of pain and touch and heat and cold.

A Way of Life

The human brain offers a nearly perfect model of transposition. Although the brain represents the "higher" point of view within the body, there is no more isolated or helpless organ. It sits in a box of thick bone, utterly dependent on lower faculties for information about the world. The brain has never seen anything, or tasted anything, or felt anything. All messages to it arrive in the same coded form, our many sensory experiences reduced down to an electrical sequence of dots and dashes (−. − −.. −. . . − −). The brain relies totally on these Morse code messages from the extremities, which it then assembles into meaning.

As I write, I am listening to Beethoven's magnificent Ninth Symphony. What is that symphony but a series of codes transposed across time and technology. It began as a musical idea which Beethoven "heard" in his mind (an extraordinary mental feat, for the composer, by then totally deaf, had only memory to guide him and could not test his idea on musical instruments). Beethoven then transposed the symphony onto paper, using a series of codes known as musical notation.

More than a century later, an orchestra read those codes, interpreted them, and reassembled them into a glorious sound approximating what Beethoven must have "heard" in his mind. Recording engineers captured that orchestra's sound as a series of magnetic impulses on a streaming tape, and a studio transposed that code into a more mechanical form, eventuating in the tiny ripples on my record album.

My turntable is now "reading" those ripples and amplifying

the variations through loudspeakers. Molecular vibrations caused by those speakers reach my ears, setting into motion another series of mechanical acts: tiny bones beat against my eardrums, transferring the vibrations through a viscous fluid on into the Organ of Corti, where 25,000 sound receptor cells lie in wait. Once stimulated, the appropriate cells fire off their electrical message. Finally, those impulses, mere dots and dashes of code, reach my brain, where the cortical screen assembles them into a sound I recognize as Beethoven's Ninth Symphony. I experience pleasure, even joy, as I pause and listen to that great work of music—the joy being once again carried to me by "lower" faculties of my body.

Transposition is a way of life. All knowledge comes to us through a process of translating downward into code and then upward into meaning. I have just written three paragraphs on Beethoven's Ninth Symphony. These were thoughts originating in my mind that I then transposed into words and typed into a computer, which recorded them in code on a magnetic disk. Eventually, my computer will transpose that magnetic code into a binary code, and a device called a modem will transpose the binary code into digital sounds that it will send over telephone wires to a publisher. If I listen in as my modem transmits the three paragraphs on Beethoven, I will hear nothing but a cloud of static, yet that static will somehow contain my thoughts and words.

The publisher's computer, receiving the digital sounds, will translate them back into magnetic codes stored on a disk. The publisher will retranslate those codes into words visible on a screen, edit them, and then transpose the words into patterned ink marks on paper—the very ink marks you are reading right now. To your trained eye, these blobs of ink on a page form letters and words that are conveyed to your eye cells and transposed into electrical impulses that your brain is assembling into some kind of meaning.

All communication, all knowledge, all sensory experience— all of life on this planet—relies on the process of transposition: meaning travels "downward" into codes which can later be reassembled. We instinctively trust that process, believing that the lower codes really do carry something of the original meaning. I trust that the words I choose, and even the staticky transmissions of my modem, will carry my original thoughts about Beethoven's Ninth Symphony. I look at a photograph, an image of the Rocky Mountains transposed on a small, flat, glossy sheet, and mentally relive a visit there. I scratch a magazine ad to smell a perfume sample, and the image of my wife, who wears that perfume, suddenly comes to mind. The lower carries something of the higher.

Transposition of the Spirit

Should it surprise us, then, to find the same universal principle operating in the realm of the spirit?

Think back to Richard's questions posed early in this book and restated at the beginning of this chapter. Why doesn't God intervene and make himself obvious? Why doesn't he speak aloud so we can hear him? We yearn for miracle, for the supernatural in its pure, unadulterated form.

I chose the word "unadulterated" deliberately because it betrays a sentiment that is central to this issue. We moderns strive to separate natural from supernatural. The natural world that we can touch and smell and see and hear seems self-evident; the supernatural world, however, is another matter. There is nothing certain about it, no skin on it, and that bothers us. We want proof. We want the supernatural to enter the natural world in a way that retains the glow, that leaves scorch marks, that rattles the ear drums.

The God revealed in the Bible does not seem to share our desire. Whereas we cleave natural from supernatural, and seen from unseen, God seeks to bring the two together. His goal, one might say, is to rescue the "lower" world, to restore the natural realm of fallen creation to its original state, where spirit and matter dwelt together in harmony.

When we become Christians and thus establish contact with the unseen world, we are not mysteriously transported upward; we do not suddenly put on space-suit bodies that remove us from the natural world (ever since the Gnostics and Manichaeans, the church has consistently judged such notions heretical). Rather, our physical bodies reconnect with spiritual reality and we begin to listen to the code through which the unseen world transposes itself into this one. One might say our task is the very opposite of reductionism. We look for ways to re-enchant or "hallow" the world: to see in nature an engine of praise, to see in bread and wine a sacrament of grace, to see in human love a shadow of ideal Love.

Granted, we have a limited vocabulary for this higher realm. We speak to God as we would speak to another person; could anything be more commonplace, more "natural"? Praying, proclaiming the gospel, meditating, fasting, offering a cup of cold water, visiting prisoners, observing the sacraments—these everyday acts, we are told, carry the "higher" meaning. They somehow express the unseen world.

Looked at from the lower, reductionist perspective, all spiritual acts have natural "explanations." Prayer is mumbling in the void; a sinner repenting, contrived emotionalism; the Day of Pentecost, an outbreak of drunkenness. A skeptic might say that the natural faculties are an impoverished lot if that's all we have to express the exalted world beyond.

But faith, looking *along* the beam, sees such natural acts as hallowed carriers of the supernatural. From that perspective, the natural world is not impoverished, but graced with miracle. And the miracle of a natural world reclaimed reached a point of climax in the Grand Miracle, when the actual Presence of God took up residence in a "natural" body exactly like ours: the Word transposed into flesh.

In one body, Christ brought the two worlds together, joining spirit and matter at long last, unifying creation in a way that had not been seen since Eden. The theologian Jürgen Moltmann puts it this way, in a sentence that merits much reflection: "Embodiment is the end of all God's works."[5] And this is how the apostle Paul puts it: "And he is the head of the body, the church. . . . For God was pleased to have all his fullness dwell in him, and through him to reconcile to himself all things, whether things on earth or things in heaven, by making peace through his blood, shed on the cross."

When that Word-become-flesh ascended, he left behind his actual Presence in the form of his body, the church. Our goodness becomes, literally, God's goodness ("Whatever you did for one of the least of these brothers of mine, you did for me"). Our suffering becomes, in Paul's words, "the fellowship of sharing in his sufferings." Our actions become his actions ("He who receives you receives me"). What happens to us, happens to him ("Saul, Saul, why do you persecute me?"). The two worlds, seen and unseen, merge in Christ; and we, as Paul kept insisting, are quite literally "in Christ." Embodiment is the end of all God's work, the goal of all creation.

From below, we tend to think of miracle as an invasion, a breaking into the natural world with spectacular force, and we long for such signs. But from above, from God's point of view, the real miracle is one of transposition: that human bodies can become vessels filled with Spirit, that ordinary human acts of charity and goodness can become nothing less than the incarnations of God on earth.

To complete the analogy, I need search no further than the words of Paul, for the image he gives to describe Christ's role in the world today is the same image I have used to illustrate transposition. Jesus Christ, said Paul, now serves as the head of the body. We know how a human head accomplishes its will: by translating orders downward in a code that the hands and eyes and mouth can understand. A healthy body is one that follows the will of the head. In that same way, the risen Christ accomplishes his will through us, members of his body.

Is God silent? I answer that question with another question: Is the church silent? We are his mouthpiece, his designated vocal chords on this planet. A plan of such awesome transposition guarantees that God's message will sometimes seem garbled or incoherent; it guarantees that God will sometimes seem silent. But embodiment was his goal, and in that light the Day of Pentecost becomes a perfect metaphor: God's voice on earth, speaking through human beings in a manner even they could not comprehend.

The Hope

I have a bright, talented, and very funny friend in Seattle named Carolyn Martin. But Carolyn has cerebral palsy, and it is the peculiar tragedy of her condition that its outward signs— drooling, floppy arm movements, inarticulate speech, a bobbing head—cause people who meet her to wonder if she is retarded. Actually, her mind is the one part of her that works perfectly; it is muscular control that she lacks.

Carolyn lived for fifteen years in a home for the mentally retarded, because the state had no other place for her. Her closest friends were people like Larry, who tore all his clothes off and ate the institution's houseplants, and Arelene, who only knew three sentences and called everyone "Mama." Carolyn determined to escape from that home and to find a meaningful place for herself in the outside world.

Eventually, she did manage to move out and establish a home of her own. There, the simplest chores posed an overwhelming challenge. It took her three months to learn to brew a pot of tea and pour it into cups without scalding herself. But Carolyn mastered that feat and many others. She enrolled in high school, graduated, then signed up for community college.

Everyone on campus knew Carolyn as "the disabled person." They would see her sitting in a wheelchair, hunched over, painstakingly typing out notes on a device called a Canon Communicator. Few felt comfortable talking with her; they could not follow her jumbled sounds. But Carolyn persevered, stretching out a two-year Associate of Arts degree program over seven years. Next, she enrolled in a Lutheran college to study the Bible. After two years there, she was asked to speak to her fellow students in chapel.

Carolyn worked many hours on her address. She typed out the final draft—at her average speed of forty-five minutes a page—and asked her friend Josee to read it for her. Josee had a strong, clear voice.

On the day of the chapel service, Carolyn sat slumped in her wheelchair on the left side of the platform. At times her arms jerked uncontrollably, her head lolled to one side so that it almost touched her shoulder, and a stream of saliva sometimes ran down her blouse. Beside her stood Josee, who read the mature and graceful prose Carolyn had composed, centered around this Bible text: "But we have this treasure in jars of clay to show that this all-surpassing power is from God but not from us."

For the first time, some students saw Carolyn as a complete human being, like themselves. Before then her mind, a very good mind, had always been inhibited by a "disobedient" body, and difficulties with speech had masked her intelligence. But hearing her address read aloud as they looked at her onstage, the students could see past the body in a wheelchair and imagine a whole person.

Carolyn told me about that day in her halting speech, and I could only understand about half the words. But the scene she described became for me a parable of transposition: a perfect mind locked inside a spastic, uncontrolled body, and vocal cords that fail at every second syllable. The New Testament image of Christ as head of the body took on new meaning as I gained a sense of both the humiliation that Christ undergoes in his role as head, and also the exaltation that he allows us, the members of his body.

We, the church, are an example of transposition taken to extreme. Sadly, we do not give off indisputable proof of God's love and glory. Sometimes, like Carolyn's body, we obscure rather than convey the message. But the church is the reason behind the entire human experiment, the reason there are human beings in the first place: to let creatures other than God bear the image of God. He deemed it well worth the risk, and the humiliation.

He who descended is the very one who ascended higher than all the heavens, in order to fill the whole universe. It was he who gave some to be apostles, some to be prophets, some to be evangelists, and some to be pastors and teachers, to prepare God's people for works of service, so that the body of Christ may be built up until we all reach unity in the faith and in the knowledge of the Son of God and become mature, attaining to the whole measure of the fullness of Christ.

Then we will no longer be infants. . . . Instead . . . we will in all things grow up into him who is the Head, that is, Christ. From him the whole body, joined and held together by every supporting ligament, grows and builds itself up in love, as each part does its work.

[1] William James, *The Varieties of Religious Experience*, 233.
[2] C. S. Lewis, *The Weight of Glory*, 18, 19.
[3] C. S. Lewis, *God in the Dock*, 212.
[4] C. S. Lewis, *Christian Reflections* 37.
[5] Jürgen Moltmann, *God in Creation*, 244.

Bible references: Colossians 1; Matthew 25; Philippians 3; Matthew 10; Acts 9; 2 Corinthians 4; Ephesians 4.

Why do you hide your face
        and consider me your enemy?
Will you torment a windblown leaf?
Will you chase after dry chaff?
                        —Job 13:24–25

Chapter 28

Is God Hidden?

T O GET the full emotional impact of Job's plight, I winnowed the book's speeches for Job's own words. I expected to find him complaining about his miserable health and lamenting the loss of his children and fortune; but to my surprise Job had relatively little to say about those matters. He focused instead on the single theme of God's absence. What hurt Job most was the sense of crying out in desperation and getting no response. I had heard that same feeling described by many suffering people, perhaps best by C. S. Lewis, who wrote these words in the midst of deep grief after his wife's death from cancer:

> Meanwhile, where is God? This is one of the most disquieting symptoms. When you are happy, so happy that you have no sense of needing Him . . . you will be—or so it feels—welcomed with open arms. But go to Him when your need is desperate, when all other help is vain, and what do you find? A door slammed in your face, and a sound of bolting and double bolting on the inside. After that, silence. You may as

well turn away. The longer you wait, the more emphatic the silence will become.[1]

Above all else, Job demanded a chance to plead his case before God. His friends' pieties he shook off like a dog shaking off fleas. He wanted the real thing, a personal appointment with God Almighty. Despite what had happened, Job could not bring himself to believe in a God of cruelty and injustice. Perhaps if they met together, at least he could hear God's side of things. But God was nowhere to be found. Job heard only the whining cant of his friends and then a dreadful, vacuous sound. The door slammed in his face.

A Fact of Faith

Oh sweet Lord, I really want to see you, I really want to be with you. . . .
                                                                          —George Harrison song

I know God is alive: I talked with him this morning!
                                                                          —bumper sticker

God loves you and has a wonderful plan for your life.
                                                                          —evangelism booklet

And he walks with me and he talks with me, and he tells me I am his own.
                                                                          —Christian hymn

Human longing for the actual presence of God may crop up almost anywhere. But we dare not make sweeping claims about the promise of God's intimate presence unless we take into account those times when God seems absent. C. S. Lewis encountered it, Job encountered it, Richard encountered it: at some point nearly everyone must face the fact of God's hiddenness.

The cloud of unknowing can descend without warning, sometimes at the very moment we most urgently desire a sense of God's presence. A South African minister, the Reverend Allan Boesak, was thrown in jail for speaking against the government.

He spent three weeks in solitary confinement, almost constantly on his knees, praying for God to set him free. "I do not mind telling you," he later related to his congregation, "that this was the most difficult moment of my life. As I knelt there, the words couldn't come anymore and there were no more tears to cry."[2] His experience was one common to blacks in South Africa: they pray, they weep, they wait, and still they provoke no answer from God.

Some would argue that God does not hide. One religious bumper sticker reads, "If you feel far from God, guess who moved?" But the guilt implicit in the slogan may be false guilt: the Book of Job details a time when, apparently, it was God who moved. Even though Job had done nothing wrong and pled desperately for help, God still chose to stay hidden. (If you ever doubt that an encounter with God's hiddenness is a normal part of the pilgrimage of faith, simply browse in a theological library among the works of the Christian mystics, men and women who have spent their lives in personal communion with God. Search for one, just one, who does not describe a time of severe testing, "the dark night of the soul.")

For those who suffer, and those who stand beside them, Job offers up an important lesson. The doubts and complaints of Meg Woodson and of Allan Boesak, and of Job, are valid responses, not symptoms of weak faith—so valid, in fact, that God made sure the Bible included them all. One does not expect to find the arguments of God's adversaries—say, Mark Twain's *Letters from the Earth* or Bertrand Russell's *Why I Am Not a Christian*—bound into the Bible, but nearly all of them make an appearance, if not in Job, then in the Psalms or Prophets. The Bible seems to anticipate our disappointments, as if God grants us in advance the weapons to use against him, as if God himself understands the cost of sustaining faith.

And, because of Jesus, perhaps he does understand. At Gethsemane and Calvary in some inexpressible way God himself was forced to confront the hiddenness of God. "God striving with God" is how Martin Luther summarized the cosmic struggle played out on two crossbeams of wood. On that dark night, God learned for himself the full extent of what it means to feel God-forsaken.

Job's friends insisted that God was not hidden. They brought up reminders—dreams, visions, past blessings, the splendors of nature—of how God had proved himself to Job in the past. "Don't forget in the darkness what you learned in the light," they chided. And those of us who live after Job have even more light: the record of fulfilled prophecy, and the life of Jesus. But sometimes all insights or "proofs" will fail. Mere memory, no matter how pleasant, will not deaden pain or loneliness. Perhaps, for a time, all verses of Scripture and all inspirational slogans will likewise fail.

Three Responses

I know too well my own instinctive response to the hiddenness of God: I retaliate by ignoring him. Like a child who thinks he can hide from adults by holding a chubby hand over his eyes, I try to shut God out of my life. If he won't reveal himself to me, why should I acknowledge him?

The Book of Job gives two other responses to such disappointment with God. The first was shown by Job's friends, who were scandalized by his assaults on the most basic tenets of their faith. Job's profound disappointment with God did not match their theology. They saw a clear-cut choice between a man who claimed to be just and a God they knew to be just. The very idea of Job demanding an audience with God! Suppress your feelings, they told him. We know for a fact that God is not unjust. So stop thinking that! Shame on you for the outrageous things you're saying!

The second response, Job's, was a rambling mess, a jarring counterpoint to his friend's relentless logic. "Why then did you bring me out of the womb?" he demanded of God. "I wish I had died before any eye ever saw me." Job lashed out in a protest he knew to be futile, like a bird repeatedly hurling itself against a windowpane. He had few sound arguments, and even admitted that his friends' logic sounded right. He wavered, contradicted himself, backtracked, and sometimes collapsed in despair. This man renowned for his righteousness railed against God: "Turn away from me so I can have a moment's joy before I go to the place of no return, to the land of gloom and deep shadow."

And which of the two responses does the book endorse? Both parties needed some correction, but after all the windy words had been uttered, God ordered the pious friends to crawl repentantly to Job and ask him to pray on their behalf.

One bold message in the Book of Job is that you can say anything to God. Throw at him your grief, your anger, your doubt, your bitterness, your betrayal, your disappointment—he can absorb them all. As often as not, spiritual giants of the Bible are shown *contending* with God. They prefer to go away limping, like Jacob, rather than to shut God out. In this respect, the Bible prefigures a tenet of modern psychology: you can't really deny your feelings or make them disappear, so you might as well express them. God can deal with every human response save one. He cannot abide the response I fall back on instinctively: an attempt to ignore him or treat him as though he does not exist. That response never once occurred to Job.

The Big Picture

Freedom to express feelings is not the only lesson from Job, however. The "behind the curtain" view of proceedings in the unseen world shows that an encounter with the hiddenness of God may badly mislead. It may tempt us to see God as the enemy and to interpret his hiddenness as a lack of concern.

Job concluded just that: "God assails me and tears me in his anger." Those of us in the audience know that Job was mistaken. For one thing, the prologue makes the subtle but important distinction that God did not personally cause Job's problems. He permitted them, yes, but the account of The Wager presents Satan, not God, as the instigator of Job's suffering. In any event, God was surely not Job's enemy. Far from being abandoned by God, Job was getting direct, almost microscopic scrutiny from him. At the very moment Job was pleading for a courtroom trial to present his case, he was actually participating in a trial of cosmic significance—not as the prosecuting attorney jabbing his finger at God, but as the main witness in a test of faith.

By no means can we infer that our own trials are, like Job's, specially arranged by God to settle some decisive issue in the universe. But we can safely assume that our limited range of vision will in similar fashion distort reality. Pain narrows vision. The most private of sensations, it forces us to think of ourselves and little else.

From Job, we can learn that much more is going on out there than we may suspect. Job felt the weight of God's absence; but a look behind the curtain reveals that in one sense God had never been more present. In the natural world, human beings only receive about 30 percent of the light spectrum. (Honeybees and homing pigeons can, for example, detect ultraviolet light waves invisible to us.) In the supernatural realm, our vision is even more limited, and we get only occasional glimpses of that unseen world.

An incident in the life of another famous Bible character makes this same point in a very different way. The prophet Daniel had a mild—mild in comparison with Job's—encounter with the hiddenness of God. Daniel puzzled over an everyday problem of unanswered prayer: why was God ignoring his repeated requests? For twenty-one days Daniel devoted himself to prayer. He mourned. He gave up choice foods. He swore off meat and wine, and used no lotions on his body. All the while he called out to God, but received no answer.

Then one day Daniel got far more than he bargained for. A supernatural being, with eyes like flaming torches and a face like lightning, suddenly showed up on a riverbank beside him. Daniel's companions all fled in terror. As for Daniel, "I had no strength left. My face turned deathly pale and I was helpless." When he tried talking to the dazzling being, he could hardly breathe.

The visitor proceeded to explain the reason for the long delay. He had been dispatched to answer Daniel's very first prayer, but had run into strong resistance from "the prince of the Persian kingdom." Finally, after a three-week standoff, reinforcements arrived and Michael, one of the chief angels, helped him break through the opposition.

Is God Hidden?

I will not attempt to interpret this amazing scene of the universe at war, except to point out a parallel to Job. Like Job, Daniel played a decisive role in the warfare between cosmic forces of good and evil, though much of the action took place beyond his range of vision. To him, prayer may have seemed futile, and God indifferent; but a glimpse "behind the curtain" reveals exactly the opposite. Daniel's limited perspective, like Job's, distorted reality.

What are we to make of Daniel's angelic being who needed reinforcements, not to mention the cosmic wager in Job? Simply this: the big picture, with the whole universe as a backdrop, includes much activity that we never see. When we stubbornly cling to God in a time of hardship, or when we simply pray, more— much more—may be involved than we ever dream. It requires faith to believe that, and faith to trust that we are never abandoned, no matter how distant God seems.

At the end, when he heard the Voice from the whirlwind, Job finally attained that faith. God reeled off natural phenomena—the solar system, constellations, thunderstorms, wild animals—that Job could not begin to explain. *If you can't comprehend the visible world you live in, how dare you expect to comprehend a world you cannot even see!* Conscious of the big picture at last, Job repented in dust and ashes.

> *God is like a person who clears his throat while hiding and so gives himself away.*
>
> —Meister Eckhardt

[1] C.S. Lewis, A Grief Observed, 9.
[2] Allan Boesak, "If You Believe," Reformed Journal, (November 1985), 11.

Bible references: Job 10, 16; Daniel 10.

I know that my Redeemer lives,
   and that in the end he will stand upon the earth.
And after my skin has been destroyed,
   yet in my flesh I will see God;
I myself will see him
   with my own eyes—I, and not another.
   How my heart yearns within me!
                                        —Job 19:25–27

Chapter 29

Why Job Died Happy

A FTER ITS ACCOUNT of tragedy and woe, of breast-beating and fierce debate, of a cosmic wager lost and won—after all that, the story of Job ends almost cozily, with Job entertaining his great-great-great-grandchildren in perfect serenity. The book gives a meticulous accounting of Job's restored fortunes: 14,000 sheep, 6000 camels, 1000 donkeys, and 10 new children.

That halcyon ending frustrates some readers, such as Elie Wiesel (Nobel Prize-winning author).[1] For him, Job had been a hero, a champion of dissent against God's injustices. Yet, says Wiesel, Job caved in. He shouldn't have let God off the hook. No amount of new prosperity could make up for the suffering Job had undergone. What of the ten children who died? No parent could believe for a moment that a bustling new brood of children would erase the sorrow of the ones Job lost.

But let Job speak for himself. This is what he said after God's majestic speech from the whirlwind:

239

> Surely I spoke of things I did not understand,
>> things too wonderful for me to know. . . .
> My ears had heard of you
>> but now my eyes have seen you.
> Therefore I despise myself
>> and repent in dust and ashes.

Evidently, what I have called God's "non-answer" satisfied Job completely.

On the other hand, some readers point to the happy ending as the final answer to disappointment with God. See, they say, God delivers his people from adversity. He restored Job's health and riches, and he will do the same for all of us if we learn to trust him as Job did. These readers, however, overlook one important detail: Job spoke his contrite words before any of his losses had been restored. He was still sitting in a pile of rubble, naked, covered with sores, and it was in *those* circumstances that he learned to praise God. Only one thing had changed: God had given Job a glimpse of the big picture.

I have a hunch that God could have said anything—could, in fact, have read from the Yellow Pages—and produced the same stunning effect on Job. What he said was not nearly so important as the mere fact of his appearance. God spectacularly answered Job's biggest question: Is anybody out there? Once Job caught sight of the unseen world, all his urgent questions faded away.

From God's viewpoint, Job's comfort was—however harsh it may sound—insignificant *in comparison with* the cosmic issues at stake. The real battle ended when Job refused to give up on God, thus causing Satan to lose The Wager. After that tough victory, God hastened to shower good gifts on Job. *Pain? I can fix that easily. More children? Camels and oxen? No problem. Of course I want you happy and wealthy and full of life! But, Job, you must understand that something far more important than happiness was at stake here.*

Of Two Worlds

My friend Richard, who still looks to Job as the most honest part of the Bible, has yet another response to its conclusion. He finds it almost irrelevant. "Job got a personal appearance by God, and I'm happy for him. That's what I've been asking for all these years. But since God hasn't visited me, how does Job help with my struggles?"

I believe that Richard has put his finger on an important dividing line of faith. In a sense, our days on earth resemble Job's *before* God came to him in a whirlwind. We too live among clues and rumors, some of which argue against a powerful, loving God. We too must exercise faith, with no certainty.

Richard lay prone on the wooden floor of his apartment, pleading for God to "reveal" himself, gambling all his faith on God's willingness to step into the seen world as he had done for Job. And Richard lost that gamble. Frankly, I doubt whether God feels any "obligation" to prove himself in such a manner. He did so many times in the Old Testament, and with finality in the person of Jesus. What further incarnations do we require of him?

I say this with great care, but I wonder if a fierce, insistent desire for miracle—even a physical healing—sometimes betrays a *lack* of faith rather than an abundance of it. Such prayers may, like Richard's, set conditions for God. When yearning for a miraculous resolution to a problem, do we make our loyalty to God contingent on whether he reveals himself yet again in the seen world?*

If we insist on visible proofs from God, we may well prepare the way for a permanent state of disappointment. True faith does not so much attempt to manipulate God to do our will as it does to position us to do his will. As I searched through the Bible for models of great faith, I was struck by how few saints experienced anything like Job's dramatic encounter with God. The rest responded to God's hiddenness not by demanding that he show himself, but by going ahead and believing him though he stayed hidden. Hebrews 11 pointedly notes that the giants of faith "did

---

*In his mercy, God may answer a prayer of mixed motives—witness all the "Lord, if you only get me out of here. . ." foxhole conversions. But that is for him to decide, not us.

not receive the things promised; they only saw them and welcomed them from a distance."

We human beings instinctively regard the seen world as the "real" world and the unseen world as the "unreal" world, but the Bible calls for almost the opposite. Through faith, the unseen world increasingly takes shape as the real world and sets the course for how we live in the seen world. Live for God, who is invisible, and not for other people, said Jesus in his words about the unseen world, or "the kingdom of heaven."

Once the apostle Paul directly addressed the question of disappointment with God. He told the Corinthians that, in spite of incredible hardships, he did not "lose heart": "Though outwardly we are wasting away, yet inwardly we are being renewed day by day. For our light and momentary [!] troubles are achieving for us an eternal glory that far outweighs them all. So we fix our eyes not on what is seen, but on what is unseen. For what is seen is temporary, but what is unseen is eternal."

A Taste of the Future

Paul endured trials and died a martyr, still anticipating his reward. Job endured trials, but received a fine reward in this life. So what, exactly, can we expect from God? Perhaps the best way to view the ending in Job is to see it not as a blueprint for what will happen to us in this life, but rather as a *sign* of what is to come. It stands as a sweet, satisfying symbol, a solution to one man's disappointment that offers us all a foretaste of the future.

In one respect, Elie Wiesel is right: the pleasures of Job's old age did not make up for the losses that had gone before. Even Job, happy and full of days, died, passing on the cycle of grief and pain to his survivors. The worst mistake of all would be to conclude that God is somehow content to make a few minor adjustments to this tragic, unfair world.

Some people stake all their faith on a miracle, as if a miracle would eliminate all disappointment with God. It wouldn't. If I had filled this book with case studies of physical healings, rather than the stories of Richard and Meg Woodson and Douglas and

Job, that would not solve the problem of disappointment with God. Something is still badly wrong with this planet. For one thing, all of us die; the ultimate mortality rate is the same for atheists and saints alike.

Miracles serve as signs pointing on to the future. They are appetizers that awaken a longing for something more, something permanent. And the happiness of Job's old age was a mere sampling of what he would enjoy after death. The good news at the end of Job and the good news of Easter at the end of the Gospels are previews of the good news described at the end of Revelation. We dare not lose sight of the world God wants.

The promise of Job 42, then, is that God will finally right the wrongs that mark our days. Some sorrows—the deaths of Job's children, for example, or the deaths of Meg Woodson's children—never heal in this life. No words of solace can assuage the grief in Meg Woodson's heart, for that grief has a precise shape, the shape of her daughter Peggie and her son Joey. But at the end of time, that grief too will vanish. Meg will get her daughter back, and her son, remade. And if I did not believe that, did not believe that Peggie and Joey Woodson are right now breathing in great gulps, and dancing, and exploring new worlds, then I would not believe anything and would have abandoned the Christian faith long ago. "If only for this life we have hope in Christ, we are to be pitied more than all men."

The Bible stakes God's reputation on his ability to conquer evil and restore heaven and earth to their original perfection. Apart from that future state, God could be judged less-than-powerful, or less-than-loving.* So far the prophets' visions of peace and justice have not come true. Swords aren't being melted into plowshares. Death, with ugly new mutations of AIDS and environmental cancers, is still swallowing people up, not being swallowed. Evil, not good, appears to be winning. But the Bible

---

*Once the Spanish mystic Unamuno, conversing with a peasant, suggested that perhaps there was a God but no heaven. The peasant thought a minute and then replied, "So what is this God for?"

calls us to see beyond the grim reality of history to the view of all eternity, when God's reign will fill the earth with light and truth.

In any discussion of disappointment with God, heaven is the last word, the most important word of all. Only heaven will finally solve the problem of God's hiddenness. For the first time ever, human beings will be able to look upon God face to face. In the midst of his agony, Job somehow came up with the faith to believe that "in my flesh I will see God; I myself will see him with my own eyes." That prophecy will come true not just for Job but for all of us.

Homesick

Many people have trouble even imagining such a future state. As Charles Williams said, "Our experience on earth makes it difficult for us to apprehend a good without a catch in it somewhere."[2] Rather than try to project ourselves into a future we can never quite grasp, perhaps we would do better to look at the unfulfilled dreams—the disappointments—of the present.

To a refugee or peasant, heaven represents a dream of a new country, a place of safety, a family reunited, a home abundant with simple things like food and fresh drinking water. (Many of the prophets spoke to refugees, which may explain why they used such earthly images.)

At some level, we all share such longings. This world may be full of pollution, war, crime, and greed, but inside us—all of us— linger remnants that remind us of what the world could be like, of what *we* could be like. You can sense such longings in the environmental movement, whose leaders yearn for a world preserved in its pristine state; and in the peace movement that dreams of a world without war; and in therapy groups that try to reconnect broken strands of love and friendship. All the beauty and joy we meet on earth represent "only the scent of a flower we have not found, the echo of a tune we have not heard, news from a country we have never yet visited."[3]

The prophets proclaim that such sensations are not illusions or mere dreams, but advance echoes of what will come true. We are given few details about that future world, only a promise that God will prove himself trustworthy. When we awake in the new heaven and new earth, we will possess at last whatever we longed for. Somehow, from all the bad news, incredible Good News emerges—a good without a catch in it somewhere. Heaven and earth will again work the way God intended. There is a happy ending after all.

Fantasy writer J. R. R. Tolkien invented a new word for this good news: it will be a "eucatastrophe," he said. A scene from his trilogy, *The Lord of the Rings*, expresses it well:

> "Is everything sad going to come untrue? What's happened to the world?" [asked Sam].
>
> "A great Shadow has departed," said Gandalf, and then he laughed, and the sound was like music, or like water in a parched land; and as he listened the thought came to him that he had not heard laughter, the pure sound of merriment, for days upon days without count. It fell upon his ears like the echo of all the joys he had ever known. But he himself burst into tears. Then, as a sweet rain will pass down a wind of spring and the sun will shine out the clearer, his tears ceased, and his laughter welled up, and laughing he sprang from his bed.
>
> "How do I feel?" he cried. "Well, I don't know how to say it. I feel, I feel"—he waved his arms in the air—"I feel like spring after winter, and sun on the leaves; and like trumpets and harps and all the songs I have ever heard!"[3]

For people who are trapped in pain, or in a broken home, or in economic misery, or in fear—for all those people, for all of us, heaven promises a time, far longer and more substantial than the time we spent on earth, of health and wholeness and pleasure and peace. If we do not believe that, then, as Paul plainly stated, there's little reason to believe at all. Without that hope, there is no hope.

The Bible never belittles human disappointment (remember the proportion in Job—one chapter of restoration follows forty-one chapters of anguish), but it does add one key word: temporary. What we feel now, we will not always feel. Our disappointment is itself a sign, an aching, a hunger for something better. And faith is, in the end, a kind of homesickness—for a home we have never visited but have never once stopped longing for.

> And the end of all our exploring
> Will be to arrive where we started
> And know the place for the first time.
> —T. S. Eliot

Then I saw a new heaven and a new earth, for the first heaven and the first earth had passed away, and there was no longer any sea. I saw the Holy City, the new Jerusalem, coming down out of heaven from God, prepared as a bride beautifully dressed for her husband. And I heard a loud voice from the throne saying, "Now the dwelling of God is with men, and he will live with them. They will be his people, and God himself will be with them and be their God. He will wipe every tear from their eyes. There will be no more death or mourning or crying or pain, for the old order of things has passed away.

[1] Elie Wiesel, *Messengers of God*, 233.
[2] Charles Williams, *The Image of the City*, 136.
[3] C. S. Lewis, *The Weight of Glory*, 5.
[4] J. R. R. Tolkien, *The Return of the King*, 283.

Bible references: Job 42; Hebrews 10; 2 Corinthians 4; 1 Corinthians 15; Job 19; Revelation 21.

Chapter 30

Two Wagers, Two Parables

Is there then any terrestrial paradise where amidst the whispering of the olive leaves people can be with whom they like and have what they like and take their ease in shadows and in coolness, or are all men's lives . . . broken, tumultuous, agonized and unromantic lives, periods punctuated by screams, by imbecilities, by deaths, by agonies?

—Ford Madox Ford, *The Good Soldier*

ITALIAN AUTHOR Umberto Eco tells of a day when, at the age of thirteen, he accompanied his father to a soccer match. Umberto did not really enjoy sports, and as he sat in the stadium observing the game his mind began to wander. "As I was observing with detachment the senseless movements down there on the field, I felt how the high noonday sun seemed to enfold men and things in a chilling light, and how before my eyes a cosmic, meaningless performance was proceeding. . . . For the first

247

time I doubted the existence of God and decided that the world was a pointless fiction."[1]

Perched high in the stadium, the adolescent Eco had imagined a viewpoint from above, like God's. But from that vantage the frantic scramblings of the human race seemed as senseless as the frantic scramblings of grown men chasing a leather ball across grass. It occurred to Eco that there must be no one "up there" watching what takes place on this planet. And if someone was there after all, he must care as little about life on earth as Umberto Eco cared about soccer.

Eco's image of the stadium raises the most basic question of faith, the question on which all else hinges: *Is anyone watching?* Are we dashing about in meaningless chaos, engulfed in "the benign indifference of the universe," or are we *performing* for Someone who cares? Job received his answer in a blinding revelation, but what about the rest of us? There is no more important question, and five years after the conversation that spawned this book I found myself discussing this question at length with my skeptical friend Richard.

When I had first met Richard, he was like an estranged lover in the early stages of separation and divorce—from God. Anger smoldered in his eyes. But when I saw him five years later, it was clear that the passage of time had mellowed him. His passion would still break out as we talked, but mingled with wistfulness, or nostalgia. He could not put God completely out of mind, and God's absence made itself felt, hauntingly, like pain from a phantom limb. Even if I didn't bring up matters of faith, Richard, still hurt, betrayed, would circle back to them.

Once he turned to me with a puzzled look. "I don't get it, Philip," he said. "We read many of the same books, and share many of the same values. You seem to understand my doubt and disappointment. And yet somehow you find it possible to believe, but I don't. What's the difference? Where did you get your faith?"

My mind sped through possible answers. I could have suggested all the evidences for God: design in creation, the story of Jesus, proofs of the Resurrection, examples of Christian saints.

But Richard knew those answers as well as I, and still did not believe. Besides, I did not get my faith from them. I got it in a dorm room in a Bible college, on a particular night in February, and so I proceeded to tell Richard about that night.

A Night of Faith

I have already mentioned that Bible college was for me, initially, a breeding ground of doubt and skepticism. I survived by learning to mimic "spiritual" behavior—a student had to, in fact, just to get good grades. There was the odious matter of "Christian service," for instance. The college required each student to participate in a regular service activity, such as street evangelism, prison ministry, or nursing home visitation. I signed up for "university work."

Every Saturday night I would visit a student center at the University of South Carolina and watch television. I was supposed to be "witnessing," of course, and the next week I would dutifully report on all the people I had approached about personal faith. My embellished stories must have sounded authentic, because no one ever questioned them.

I was also required to attend a weekly prayer meeting with four other students involved in university work. Those meetings followed a consistent pattern: Joe would pray, and then Craig, and Chris, and the other Joe, and then all four would pause politely for about ten seconds. I never prayed; and after the brief silence, we would open our eyes and return to our rooms.

But one February night to everyone's surprise, including my own, I did pray. I have no idea why. I had not planned to. But after Joe and Craig and Chris and Joe had finished, I found myself praying aloud. "God," I said, and I could sense the tension level in the room rise.

As I recall it, I said something like this: "God, here we are, supposed to be concerned about those ten thousand students at the University of South Carolina who are going to hell. Well, you know that I don't care if they all go to hell, if there is one. I don't even care if I go to there."

You would have to attend a Bible college to appreciate how these words must have sounded to the others in the room. I may as well have been invoking witchcraft or offering child sacrifices. But no one stirred or tried to stop me, and I continued praying.

For some reason, I started talking about the parable of the Good Samaritan. We Bible college types were supposed to feel the same concern for university students as the Samaritan felt for the bloodied Jew lying in the ditch. But I felt no such concern, I said. I felt nothing for them.

And then it happened. In the middle of my prayer, just as I was describing how little I cared for our assigned targets of compassion, I saw that story in a new light. I had been visualizing the scene as I spoke: an old-fashioned-looking Samaritan, dressed in robes and a turban, bending over a dirty, blood-crusted form in a ditch. But suddenly, in the internal screen of my brain, those two figures changed. The kindly Samaritan took on the face of Jesus. The Jew, pitiable victim of a highway robbery, took on another face too—a face I recognized with a start as my own.

In a flash I saw Jesus reaching down with a moistened rag to clean my wounds and stanch the flow of blood. And as he bent over, I saw myself, the wounded robbery victim, open my eyes and purse my lips. Then, as if watching in slow motion, I saw myself spit at him, full in the face. I saw all that—I, who did not believe in visions, or in biblical parables, or even in Jesus. It stunned me. Abruptly, I stopped praying, got up, and left the room.

All that evening I thought about what had happened. It wasn't exactly a vision—more like a daydreamed parable with a moral twist. Still, I couldn't put it behind me. What did it mean? Was it genuine? I wasn't sure, but I knew that my cockiness had been shattered. On that campus I had always found security in my agnosticism. No longer. I had caught a new glimpse of myself. Perhaps in all my self-assured and mocking skepticism I was the neediest one of all.

I wrote a brief note to my fiancée that night, saying

guardedly, "I want to wait a few days before talking about it, but I may have just had the first authentic religious experience of my life."

Two Wagers

I told that story to Richard, who listened with genuine interest. Everything in my life had changed from that moment on, I said. Before then, if anyone had suggested I would spend my life writing about the Christian faith, I would have thought him insane. But since that February night I have been on a slow, steady pilgrimage to reclaim what I had once rejected as religious nonsense. I received eyes of faith that opened up belief in the unseen world.

Richard was kind, but unconvinced. He pointed out gently that there were, after all, alternative explanations for what had happened. For several years I had been resisting a fundamentalist upbringing, and undoubtedly that repression had caused a deep "cognitive dissonance" within me. Since I had not prayed for so long, should it surprise me that my first prayer, no matter how tentative, would release a flood of emotions that might find an outlet in such form as the "revelation" of the Good Samaritan parable?

I had to smile as Richard talked, because I recognized myself in his words. I had used that same language to explain away the personal testimonies of scores of my fellow students. But ever since that night in February I have seen things differently.

Richard and I were describing the same phenomenon two different ways: he was looking "at the beam," while I was looking along it. He had certain evidence on his side. I had certain evidence on mine—mainly the profound and unexpected change in my outlook on life. But conversions only make sense from the inside out, to the fellow-converted. We were back where we had started in our conversation five years before: we had arrived at the mystery of *faith*, a word Richard detested.

I found myself wishing I could make faith crystal clear for him, but I felt powerless to do so. I sensed in Richard the same restlessness and alienation that I had lived with, and that God had gradually healed. But I could not transplant faith into Richard; he must exercise it for himself.

It was during this conversation that I realized there are actually two cosmic wagers transpiring. I have focused on The Wager from God's point of view, The Wager as pictured in the Book of Job, in which God "risks" the future of the human experiment on a person's response. I doubt anyone fully understands that wager, but Jesus taught that the end of human history will boil down to the one issue: "When the Son of Man comes, will he find faith on the earth?"

The second wager, reflecting the human viewpoint, is the one that Job himself engaged in: should he choose for God or against him? Job weighed the evidence, most of which did not suggest a trustworthy God. But he decided, kicking and screaming all the way, to place his faith in God.

Each one of us must choose whether to live as if God exists, or as if he does not exist. When Umberto Eco sat high in the stadium under a noonday sun and looked down on a field of soccer players, he seized upon the most important question of his life—of any life. Is anyone watching? And the answer to that question rests squarely upon faith—by that and only that the just shall live.

Two Parables

I end this book with two stories, both of them true, which for me stand as parables for the alternatives: the way of faith and the way of non-faith.

The first comes from a sermon by Frederick Buechner:

> It is a peculiarly twentieth-century story, and it is almost too awful to tell: about a boy of twelve or thirteen who, in a fit of crazy anger and depression, got hold of a gun somewhere and fired it at his father, who died not right away but soon afterward. When the authorities asked the boy why he had done it, he said that it was because he could not stand his father, because his father demanded too much of him, because he was always after him, because he hated his father. And

252

then later on, after he had been placed in a house of detention somewhere, a guard was walking down the corridor late one night when he heard sounds from the boy's room, and he stopped to listen. The words that he heard the boy sobbing out in the dark were, "I want my father, I want my father."[1]

Buechner says that this story is "a kind of parable of the lives of all of us." Modern society is like that boy in the house of detention. We have killed off our Father. Few thinkers or writers or moviemakers or television producers take God seriously anymore. He's an anachronism, something we've outgrown. The modern world has accepted The Wager and bet against God. There are too many unanswered questions. He has disappointed us once too often. *

It is a hard thing to live, uncertain of anything. And yet, sobs can still be heard, muffled cries of loss, such as those expressed in literature and film and almost all modern art. The alternative to disappointment with God seems to be disappointment without God. ("The center of me," said Bertrand Russell, "is always and eternally a terrible pain—a curious wild pain—a searching for something beyond what the world contains.")

I see that sense of loss in the eyes of my friend Richard, even now. He says he does not believe in God, but he keeps bringing up the subject, protesting too loudly. From where comes this wounded sense of betrayal if no one is there to do the betraying?

Frederick Buechner's parable concerns the loss of a father; the second concerns the discovery of a father. It too is a true story, my own story.

---

* "Have you not heard of the man who lit a lamp on a bright morning and went to the marketplace crying ceaselessly, 'I seek God. I seek God'. . . . They laughed, and . . . the man sprang into their midst and looked daggers at them. 'Where is God?' he cried. 'I will tell you. We have killed Him, you and I.' We are all His killers, but how can we have done that? How could we swallow up the sea? Who gave us the sponge to wipe away the horizon? What will we do as the earth is set loose from its sun?"—Friedrich Nietzsche, *The Gay Science*

One holiday I was visiting my mother, who lives seven hundred miles away. We reminisced about times long past, as mothers and sons tend to do. Inevitably, the large box of old photos came down from the closet shelf, spilling out a jumbled pile of thin rectangles that mark my progression through childhood and adolescence: the cowboy-and-Indian getups, the Peter Cottontail suit in the first grade play, my childhood pets, endless piano recitals, the graduations from grade school and high school and finally college.

Among those photos I found one of an infant, with my name written on the back. The portrait itself was not unusual. I looked like any baby: fat-cheeked, half-bald, with a wild, unfocused look to my eyes. But the photo was crumpled and mangled, as if one of those childhood pets had got hold of it. I asked my mother why she had hung onto such an abused photo when she had so many other undamaged ones.

There is something you should know about my family: when I was ten months old, my father contracted spinal lumbar polio. He died three months later, just after my first birthday. My father was totally paralyzed at age twenty-four, his muscles so weakened that he had to live inside a large steel cylinder that did his breathing for him. He had few visitors—people had as much hysteria about polio in 1950 as they do about AIDS today. The one visitor who came faithfully, my mother, would sit in a certain place so that he could see her in a mirror bolted to the side of the iron lung.

My mother explained to me that she had kept the photo as a memento, because during my father's illness it had been fastened to his iron lung. He had asked for pictures of her and of his two sons, and my mother had had to jam the pictures in between some metal knobs. Thus, the crumpled condition of my baby photo.

I rarely saw my father after he entered the hospital, since children were not allowed in polio wards. Besides, I was so young that, even if I had been allowed in, I would not now retain those memories.

When my mother told me the story of the crumpled photo, I had a strange and powerful reaction. It seemed odd to imagine someone caring about me whom, in a sense, I had never met.

254

During the last months of his life, my father had spent his waking hours staring at those three images of his family, my family. There was nothing else in his field of view. What did he do all day? Did he pray for us? Yes, surely. Did he love us? Yes. But how can a paralyzed person express his love, especially when his own children are banned from the room?

I have often thought of that crumpled photo, for it is one of the few links connecting me to the stranger who was my father, a stranger who died a decade younger than I am now. Someone I have no memory of, no sensory knowledge of, spent all day every day thinking of me, devoting himself to me, loving me as well as he could. Perhaps, in some mysterious way, he is doing so now in another dimension. Perhaps I will have time, much time, to renew a relationship that was cruelly ended just as it had begun.

I mention this story because the emotions I felt when my mother showed me the crumpled photo were the very same emotions I felt that February night in a college dorm room when I first believed in a God of love. *Someone is there*, I realized. Someone is watching life as it unfolds on this planet. More, Someone is there who loves me. It was a startling feeling of wild hope, a feeling so new and overwhelming that it seemed fully worth risking my life on.

[1]Umberto Eco, *Travels in Hyper Reality*, 167-168.
[2]Frederick Buechner, *The Magnificent Defeat*, 65.

Bible reference: Luke 18.

Thanks

SOMEDAY I may have to write a book on my own, but I hope that time doesn't come soon because I now rely very heavily on the editorial suggestions of other readers. I am hopelessly and gratefully dependent on my friend Tim Stafford, who read this manuscript in three successive drafts. That was a labor of love: before Tim's expert suggestions on needed cuts, the manuscript was fifty percent longer.

I also had the good fortune of participating in a manuscript evaluation session with four other writers—Steve Lawhead, Karen Mains, Luci Shaw, and Walter Wangerin, Jr.—who helped me set the tone for the final draft. Then in separate sessions Walter unveiled to me some of the mysteries of storytelling. And these others also read and critiqued the manuscript, giving me valuable advice: Elsie Baker, Dr. John Boyle, Dr. Paul Brand, Harold Fickett, Hal Knight, Lee Phillips, and Dr. Cornelius Plantinga.

After I had acted on all these folks' advice, Judith Markham, my editor on three previous books, edited the final result. Judith offers a rare combination of diplomacy, literary wisdom, kindness, and, above all, a pursuit of excellence. She is a good friend, and a fine editor.

Some names—Augustine, Buechner, Chesterton, Eliot, Lewis, Moltmann, MacDonald, Pascal, Sayers, Thielicke, and Williams—you have already met, for they appear throughout the book. In the truest sense, they are my "pastors." Because of them, in no small measure, I continue to believe.

A class I taught at LaSalle Street Church assured that for at least five years I would study the Old Testament in detail, and its members contributed many fine insights and daunting questions.

I referred several times to an inspiring visit to the Colorado mountains: I'm grateful to the Konemans and the Braytons, who made that time possible.

And I want to thank Richard. He has the courage to be honest; I have learned much from him. I hope that he never stops asking questions, that he never abandons his search.

Bibliography

Augustine, Saint. *The Confessions of Saint Augustine.* Translated by John K. Ryan. Garden City: Doubleday, 1960.

Brown, Colin. *Miracles and the Critical Mind.* Grand Rapids: Eerdmans, 1984.

Buechner, Frederick. *The Hungering Dark.* New York: Seabury, 1981.

_____. *The Magnificent Defeat.* New York: Seabury, 1979.

_____. *A Room Called Remember: Uncollected Pieces.* New York: Harper & Row, 1984.

_____. *Wishful Thinking: A Theological ABC.* Harper & Row, 1973.

Dostoyevsky, Fyodor. *The Brothers Karamazov.* Garden City: Nelson Doubleday (no date).

Eco, Umberto. *Travels in Hyper Reality: Essays.* Edited by Helen & Kurt Wolff. Translated from the Italian by William Weaver. New York: Harcourt Brace Jovanovich, 1983.

Eiseley, Loren. *The Star Thrower.* Harcourt Brace Jovanovich, 1979.

Hall, Douglas John. *God and Human Suffering.* Minneapolis: Augsburg, 1986.

James, William. *The Varieties of Religious Experience.* New York: Modern Library, 1936.

Kierkegaard, Søren. *Philosophical Fragments*. Translated by David Swenson. Princeton: Princeton University Press, 1962.

Lewis, C. S. *Christian Reflections*. Grand Rapids: Eerdmans, 1974.

———. *God in the Dock*. Edited by Walter Hooper. Grand Rapids: Eerdmans, 1970.

———. *A Grief Observed*. New York: Seabury, 1961.

———. *The Weight of Glory and Other Addresses*. Grand Rapids: Eerdmans, 1975.

———. *The World's Last Night and Other Essays*. New York: Harcourt Brace Jovanovich, Inc., 1959.

MacDonald, George. *Life Essential: The Hope of the Gospel*. Edited by Rolland Hein. Wheaton, Ill.: Harold Shaw, 1978.

MacDonald, Greville. *George MacDonald and His Wife*. London: George Allen and Unwin, Ltd., 1924.

Moltmann, Jürgen. *God in Creation: A New Theology of Creation and the Spirit of God*. New York: Harper & Row, 1985.

Spark, Muriel. *The Only Problem*. New York: Putnam, 1984.

Thompson, William I. *The Time Falling Bodies Take to Light*. New York: St. Martin's Press, 1982.

Tolkien, J. R. R. *The Return of the King*. New York: Ballantine, 1976.

———. *The Tolkien Reader*. New York: Ballantine Books, 1966.

Wiesel, Elie. *Messengers of God: Biblical Portraits and Legends*. New York: Summit Books, 1985.

Williams, Charles. *He Came Down from Heaven*. London: William Heinemann, Ltd., 1938.

———. *The Image of the City*. London: Oxford University Press, 1958.